A Gift to

_____

From

_____

Date

_____

THE GREATEST BIBLE PROMISES

FOR FAITH & MIRACLES

SMITH**WIGGLESWORTH**

WHITAKER
HOUSE

The Greatest Bible Promises for Faith and Miracles

ISBN: 978-1-62911-868-0
eBook ISBN: 978-1-62911-871-0
Printed in the United States of America
© 2017 by Whitaker House

Whitaker House
1030 Hunt Valley Circle
New Kensington, PA 15068
www.whitakerhouse.com

Library of Congress Cataloging-in-Publication Data (Pending)

1 2 3 4 5 6 7 8 9 10 **UJ** 23 22 21 20 19 18 17

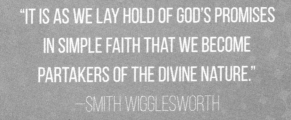

"IT IS AS WE LAY HOLD OF GOD'S PROMISES
IN SIMPLE FAITH THAT WE BECOME
PARTAKERS OF THE DIVINE NATURE."
—SMITH WIGGLESWORTH

CONTENTS

A Word from the Editor 11

Let Me Say a Word to Your Hearts 13

CHAPTER ONE: FAITH TO TRUST GOD...

For Confidence 17

In Conflict 19

For Courage 21

In Discouragement... 23

In Failure 25

In Fear.. 26

For God's Care... 29

For God's Grace 32

For God's Favor 35

For Guidance 36

For Healing..39

CHAPTER TWO: THE LIVING POWER OF FAITH TO...

Overcome Anger 45

Relieve Anxiety.. 46

Defeat Depression.. 49

Conquer Doubt 52

Help During Trouble 53

Activate Faith 56

Receive God's Love.. 60

Pray Expectantly 64

Vanquish Pride 68

Abolish Worry... 69

CHAPTER THREE: DARE TO BELIEVE

Belief in Jesus 73

Blessings 75

Correction 78

Desert Places...79

Destroying Strongholds 80

Encouragement... 82

God's Favor 86

Finding God in Hard Times.. 88

God's Presence.. 90

Joy & Gladness 94

Patience... 96

Provision Gifts.. 98

Times of Uncertainty 99

CHAPTER FOUR: POWER OF FAITH IN SCRIPTURE

Faith in God's Power 103

Faith in God's Words 106

Faith in Jesus' Name 110

Accounts of Faith in Scripture..................................... 112

Power of Scripture 120

CHAPTER FIVE: A LIVING FAITH

Accepting Others 133

Ambition 135

Calling.. 137

Change 141

Character... 143

Commitment 145

Confession.. 146

Contentment.. 147

Deceit 150

Discipleship.. 151

Goals 153

Mercy 155

Trust.. 158

CHAPTER SIX: THE WAY OF FAITH

Assurance 163

Control Over Sin.. 168

Control Over Temptation................................ 169

Dependence... 171

Future.. 173

Giving.. 175

Heaven 177

Hope 179

Walking with God... 183

CHAPTER SEVEN: MIRACLE POWER OF FAITH

Breakthrough... 193

Faithfulness... 197

Healing 201

Faith for Miracles... 204

Power for Miracles 210

Receiving a Miracle 214

My Favorite Bible Promises 218

A WORD FROM THE EDITOR

The Greatest Bible Promises is a collection of God's promises in Scripture, from the *King James Version Easy Read Bible* (KJVER), combined with beloved quotes from the various writings of the Apostle of Faith, Smith Wigglesworth (1859–1947).

An encounter with Smith Wigglesworth was an unforgettable experience. This seems to be the universal reaction of all who knew him or heard him speak. Wigglesworth was a simple yet remarkable man who was used by God in extraordinary ways. He had a contagious and inspiring faith. Under his ministry, thousands of people came to salvation, committed themselves to a deeper faith in Christ, received the baptism in the Holy Spirit, and were miraculously healed. The power that brought these kinds of results was the presence of the Holy Spirit, who filled Smith Wigglesworth and used him in bringing the good news of the gospel to people all over the world. Wigglesworth gave glory to God for everything that was accomplished through his ministry, and he wanted people to understand his work only in this context, because his sole desire was that people would see Jesus and not himself.

It is our hope that by reading Wigglesworth's words of wisdom and inspiration combined with the wonderful promises found in Scripture, you will truly experience the divine presence of our miraculous God and take to heart one of Wigglesworth's favorite sayings: "Only believe!"

LET ME SAY A WORD TO YOUR HEARTS...

If any of you lack wisdom, let him ask of God, that gives to all men liberally, and upbraids not; and it shall be given him. But let him ask in faith, nothing wavering. For he that wavers is like a wave of the sea driven with the wind and tossed.
—JAMES 1:5–6

This is a living word of faith: *"If any of you lacks wisdom, let him ask of God, that gives to all men liberally."* You will never find that God ever judges you for the wisdom He gives you or for the blessing He gives you. He makes it so that when you come to Him again, He gives again, never asking what you did with what He gave you before. That is the way God gives. God *"gives to all men liberally, and upbraids not."* So you have a chance today to come for much more. Do you want wisdom? Ask of God.

Dear believer, the trial of your faith is much more precious than gold that perishes. When God so purifies you through trials, misunderstandings, persecution, and suffering because you are wrongfully judged, because you have not believed what people say to you, Jesus has given you the keynote: rejoice in that day.

As you are tested in the fire, the Master is cleaning away everything that cannot bring out the image of Him in you. He is cleaning away all the dross from your life, and every evil power, until He sees His face right in the life, until He sees His face right in your life.

In God's Word, there is always more to follow, always more to know. If only we could be like children in taking in the mind of God, what wonderful things would happen. Do you apply the whole Bible to your life? It is grand. Never mind those who take only a part. You take it all. When we get such a thirst that nothing can satisfy us but God, we will have a royal time.

The child of God must have reality all the time. After the child of God comes into the sweetness of the perfume of the presence of God, he will have the hidden treasures of God. He will always be feeding on that blessed truth that will make life full of glory. Are you dry? There is no dry place in God, but all good things come out of hard times.

The harder the place you are in, the more blessing can come out of it as you yield to His plan. Oh, if only I had known God's plan in its fullness, I might never have had a tear in my life. God is so abundant, so full of love and mercy; there is no lack to those who trust in Him. I pray that God will give us a touch of reality, so that we may be able to trust Him all the way.

Are you ready? What for? To come to a place where you will not give way, where you will dare believe that God is the same today and will surely make you satisfied because He longs to fill you. Those who believe will be satisfied.

Are you ready? What for? That you may so apply your heart to the will of God, so yield yourself to His purposes, that God will have a plan through your life that never before has been.

Are you ready? What for? That today you may so come into like-mindedness with Christ, that you may have no more human desire but will be cut short from all human bondages and set free. The shoreline must never know you more. Come to God in all His fullness, His revelation, His power, that you may be clothed upon with God today.

—*Smith Wigglesworth*

"FEAR LOOKS; FAITH JUMPS. FAITH NEVER FAILS TO OBTAIN ITS OBJECT. IF I LEAVE YOU AS I FOUND YOU, I AM NOT GOD'S CHANNEL. I AM NOT HERE TO ENTERTAIN YOU, BUT TO GET YOU TO THE PLACE WHERE YOU CAN LAUGH AT THE IMPOSSIBLE."

—SMITH WIGGLESWORTH

1

FAITH TO TRUST GOD...

FOR CONFIDENCE

It is better to trust in the Lord *than to put confidence in man. It is better to trust in the* Lord *than to put confidence in princes.*
PSALM 118:8–9

Both young men, and maidens; old men, and children: let them praise the name of the Lord: *for His name alone is excellent; His glory is above the earth and heaven.* PSALM 148:12–13

My son, forget not my law; but let your heart keep my commandments: for length of days, and long life, and peace, shall they add to you. PROVERBS 3:1–2

For the Lord *shall be your confidence, and shall keep your foot from being taken.* PROVERBS 3:26

In the fear of the Lord *is strong confidence: and his children shall have a place of refuge.* PROVERBS 14:26

Let us draw near with a true heart in full assurance of faith, having our hearts sprinkled from an evil conscience, and our bodies washed with pure water. HEBREWS 10:22

Cast not away therefore your confidence, which has great recompence of reward. HEBREWS 10:35

My brethren, count it all joy when you fall into divers temptations; knowing this, that the trying of your faith works patience. But let patience have her perfect work, that you may be perfect and entire, wanting nothing. JAMES 1:2–4

And hereby we know that we are of the truth, and shall assure our hearts before Him. For if our heart condemn us, God is greater than our heart, and knows all things. Beloved, if our heart condemn us not, then have we confidence toward God.

1 JOHN 3:19–21

He that has the Son has life; and he that has not the Son of God has not life. These things have I written to you that believe on the name of the Son of God; that you may know that you have eternal life, and that you may believe on the name of the Son of God.

1 JOHN 5:12–13

IN CONFLICT

A soft answer turns away wrath: but grievous words stir up anger.   PROVERBS 15:1

Make no friendship with an angry man; and with a furious man you shall not go: lest you learn his ways, and get a snare to your soul.   PROVERBS 22:24–25

But I say to you, Love your enemies, bless them that curse you, do good to them that hate you, and pray for them which despitefully use you, and persecute you.   MATTHEW 5:44

Charity suffers long, and is kind; charity envies not; charity vaunts not itself, is not puffed up, does not behave itself unseemly, seeks not her own, is not easily provoked, thinks no evil.
                    1 CORINTHIANS 13:4–5

Be you angry, and sin not: let not the sun go down upon your wrath: neither give place to the devil.   EPHESIANS 4:26–27

Wherefore, my beloved brethren, let every man be swift to hear, slow to speak, slow to wrath: for the wrath of man works not the righteousness of God.   JAMES 1:19–20

INSIGHTS ON FAITH FROM SMITH WIGGLESWORTH

There is a rest of faith; there is a faith that rests in confidence on God. God's promises never fail. "Faith comes by hearing, and hearing by the word of God." The Word of God can create an irresistible faith, a faith that is never daunted, a faith that never gives up and never fails.

⌒

If we are in a place of substance, of reality, of ideal purpose, it is not human; we are dealing with almightiness. I have a present God, I have a living faith, and the living faith is the Word. The Word is life, and the Word is equipment, and the Lord is "the same yesterday, today, and forever."

⌒

All lack of faith is due to not feeding on God's Word. You need it every day. How can you enter into a life of faith? Feed on the living Christ of whom this Word is full. As you are taken up with the glorious fact and the wondrous presence of the living Christ, the faith of God will spring up within you. "Faith comes by hearing, and hearing by the word of God."

FOR COURAGE

Be strong and of a good courage, fear not, nor be afraid of them: for the LORD your God, He it is that does go with you; He will not fail you, nor forsake you. DEUTERONOMY 31:6

Only be you strong and very courageous, that you may observe to do according to all the law, which Moses My servant commanded you: turn not from it to the right hand or to the left, that you may prosper wherever you go. JOSHUA 1:7

I go the way of all the earth: be you strong therefore, and show yourself a man; and keep the charge of the LORD your God, to walk in His ways, to keep His statutes, and His commandments, and His judgments, and His testimonies, as it is written in the law of Moses, that you may prosper in all that you do, and wherever you turn yourself. 1 KINGS 2:2–3

He gives power to the faint; and to them that have no might He increases strength. ISAIAH 40:29

When you pass through the waters, I will be with you; and through the rivers, they shall not overflow you: when you walk through the fire, you shall not be burned; neither shall the flame kindle upon you. ISAIAH 43:2

I will love You, O LORD, my strength. The LORD is my rock, and my fortress, and my deliverer; my God, my strength, in whom I will trust; my buckler, and the horn of my salvation, and my high tower. PSALM 18:1–2

Wait on the LORD: be of good courage, and He shall strengthen your heart: wait, I say, on the LORD. PSALM 27:14

Be of good courage, and He shall strengthen your heart, all you that hope in the LORD. PSALM 31:24

Trust in the LORD, and do good; so shall you dwell in the land, and verily you shall be fed. PSALM 37:3

But right away Jesus spoke to them, saying, Be of good cheer; it is I; be not afraid. MATTHEW 14:27

And Jesus answering said to them, Have faith in God. MARK 11:22

So that we may boldly say, The LORD is my helper, and I will not fear what man shall do to me. HEBREWS 13:6

IN DISCOURAGEMENT

Behold, the LORD *your God has set the land before you: go up and possess it, as the* LORD *God of your fathers has said to you; fear not, neither be discouraged.* DEUTERONOMY 1:21

Have not You made an hedge about him, and about his house, and about all that he has on every side? You have blessed the work of his hands, and his substance is increased in the land. JOB 1:10

As the mountains are round about Jerusalem, so the LORD *is round about His people from here after even for ever.* PSALM 125:2

O GOD *the Lord, the strength of my salvation, You have covered my head in the day of battle.* PSALM 140:7

A merry heart does good like a medicine: but a broken spirit dries the bones. PROVERBS 17:22

But they that wait upon the LORD *shall renew their strength; they shall mount up with wings as eagles; they shall run, and not be weary; and they shall walk, and not faint.* ISAIAH 40:31

INSIGHTS ON FAITH FROM SMITH WIGGLESWORTH

You ask, "What is faith?" Faith is the principle of the Word of God. The Holy Spirit, who inspired the Word, is called the Spirit of Truth. As we *"receive with meekness the implanted word,"* faith springs up in our hearts—faith in the sacrifice of Calvary; faith in the shed blood of Jesus; faith in the fact that He took our weaknesses, bore our sicknesses, carried our pains, and is our life today.

⌒

Faith is actively refusing the power of the Devil. It is not saying mere words. You must have an activity of faith, refusing the conditions in the name of Jesus. We must have something more than words. Satan comes *"to kill, and to destroy"* (John 10:10). Jesus comes to give life abundantly. He comes to give abounding life through the operation of the Holy Spirit.

⌒

There are three things that work together. The first is faith. Faith can always bring the second thing—a fact—and a fact can always bring the third thing—joy. So God brings you to hear the Scriptures, which can make you wise unto salvation (2 Tim. 3:15), which can open your understanding and make you so that if you will hear the truth, you will go out with what you want.

IN FAILURE

And David said to Solomon his son, Be strong and of good courage, and do it: fear not, nor be dismayed: for the LORD God, even my God, will be with you; He will not fail you, nor forsake you, until you have finished all the work for the service of the house of the LORD. 1 CHRONICLES 28:20

I will lift up my eyes to the hills, from where comes my help. My help comes from the LORD, which made heaven and earth.
PSALM 121:1–2

The LORD is good, a strong hold in the day of trouble; and He knows them that trust in Him. NAHUM 1:7

And be not conformed to this world: but be you transformed by the renewing of your mind, that you may prove what is that good, and acceptable, and perfect, will of God.
ROMANS 12:2

For we have not an high priest which cannot be touched with the feeling of our infirmities; but was in all points tempted like as we are, yet without sin. Let us therefore come boldly to the throne of grace, that we may obtain mercy, and find grace to help in time of need. HEBREWS 4:15–16

IN FEAR

The LORD is my light and my salvation; whom shall I fear? the LORD is the strength of my life; of whom shall I be afraid? When the wicked, even my enemies and my foes, came upon me to eat up my flesh, they stumbled and fell. Though a host should encamp against me, my heart shall not fear: though war should rise against me, in this will I be confident. PSALM 27:1–3

He shall cover you with His feathers, and under His wings shall you trust: His truth shall be your shield and buckler. You shall not be afraid for the terror by night; nor for the arrow that flies by day; nor for the pestilence that walks in darkness; nor for the destruction that wastes at noonday. PSALM 91:4–6

But whoso hearkens to me shall dwell safely, and shall be quiet from fear of evil. PROVERBS 1:33

When you lie down, you shall not be afraid: yea, you shall lie down, and your sleep shall be sweet. PROVERBS 3:24

And it shall come to pass in the day that the LORD shall give you rest from your sorrow, and from your fear, and from the hard bondage wherein you were made to serve. ISAIAH 14:3

For I the LORD your God will hold your right hand, saying to you, Fear not; I will help you. ISAIAH 41:13

I, even I, am He that comforts you: who are you, that you should be afraid of a man that shall die, and of the son of man which shall be made as grass. ISAIAH 51:12

In righteousness shall you be established: you shall be far from oppression; for you shall not fear: and from terror; for it shall not come near you. ISAIAH 54:14

Fear not, little flock; for it is your Father's good pleasure to give you the kingdom. LUKE 12:32

For you have not received the spirit of bondage again to fear; but you have received the Spirit of adoption, whereby we cry, Abba, Father. ROMANS 8:15

Nay, in all these things we are more than conquerors through Him that loved us. For I am persuaded, that neither death, nor life, nor angels, nor principalities, nor powers, nor things present, nor things to come, nor height, nor depth, nor any other creature, shall be able to separate us from the love of God, which is in Christ Jesus our Lord. ROMANS 8:37–39

INSIGHTS ON FAITH FROM SMITH WIGGLESWORTH

It is a great thing to know that God is loosing you from the world, loosing you from a thousand things. You must seek to have the mind of God in all things. If you don't, you will stop His working.

⌒

Faith is the substance, and it is a reality. God wants to bring us to the fact of it. He wants us to know that we have something greater than we can see or handle, because everything we can see and handle is going to pass away. The heavens are going to be wrapped up, the earth will melt with fervent heat, but the Word of the Lord will abide forever.

⌒

You will find that there is no peace, no help, no source of strength, no power, no life, nothing that can satisfy the cry of the child of God but the Word of God. God has a special way of satisfying the cry of His children. He is waiting to open to us the windows of heaven until He has so moved in the depths of our hearts that everything unlike Himself has been destroyed.

FOR GOD'S CARE

But You, O LORD, are a shield for me; my glory, and the lifter up of my head. PSALM 3:3

The LORD is my shepherd; I shall not want. He makes me to lie down in green pastures: He leads me beside the still waters. He restores my soul: He leads me in the paths of righteousness for His name's sake. PSALM 23:1–3

Delight yourself also in the LORD: and He shall give you the desires of your heart. PSALM 37:4

Bless the LORD, O my soul, and forget not all His benefits: who forgives all your iniquities; who heals all your diseases; who redeems your life from destruction; who crowns you with loving-kindness and tender mercies; who satisfies your mouth with good things; so that your youth is renewed like the eagle's. PSALM 103:2–5

I love the LORD, because He has heard my voice and my supplications. PSALM 116:1

O LORD, You have searched me, and known me. You know my downsitting and my uprising, You understand my thought afar off. You compass my path and my lying down, and are acquainted with all my ways. PSALM 139:1–3

It is of the Lord's mercies that we are not consumed, because His compassions fail not. They are new every morning: great is your faithfulness. The Lord is my portion, says my soul; therefore will I hope in Him. The Lord is good to them that wait for Him, to the soul that seeks Him. It is good that a man should both hope and quietly wait for the salvation of the Lord.

LAMENTATIONS 3:22–26

Are not two sparrows sold for a farthing? and one of them shall not fall on the ground without your Father. But the very hairs of your head are all numbered. Fear you not therefore, you are of more value than many sparrows. MATTHEW 10:29–31

For I will give you a mouth and wisdom, which all your adversaries shall not be able to gainsay nor resist. LUKE 21:15

He that spared not His own Son, but delivered Him up for us all, how shall He not with Him also freely give us all things?

ROMANS 8:32

Not that we are sufficient of ourselves to think any thing as of ourselves; but our sufficiency is of God. 2 CORINTHIANS 3:5

Blessed be the God and Father of our Lord Jesus Christ, who has blessed us with all spiritual blessings in heavenly places in Christ. EPHESIANS 1:3

INSIGHTS ON FAITH FROM SMITH WIGGLESWORTH

The greatest weakness in the world is unbelief. The greatest power is the faith that works by love. Love, mercy, and grace are bound eternally to faith. Fear is the opposite of faith, but *"there is no fear in love"* (1 John 4:18). Those whose hearts are filled with a divine faith and love have no question in their hearts as to being caught up when Jesus comes.

⌒

Now God does not want anybody in the world, under any circumstances, to be in a place where he lives on eyesight and on feelings. Faith never looks and faith never feels. Faith is an act, and faith without an act is not faith, but doubt and disgrace. Every one of you has more faith than you are using.

⌒

The Word of God cannot fail, because it is the living Word. Listen to the words of Jesus as He says, *"Greater works than these* [you] *will do"* (John 14:12). I know as truly as I stand upon this platform that we will see the rising tide of blessing and divine healing go forth with greater power. But Satan will always try to hinder the real work of God. Whenever the power of God is being manifested, Satan will be there trying to upset it.

FOR GOD'S GRACE

For if you turn again to the LORD, your brethren and your children shall find compassion before them that lead them captive, so that they shall come again into this land: for the LORD your God is gracious and merciful, and will not turn away His face from you, if you return to Him.   2 CHRONICLES 30:9

He has not dealt with us after our sins; nor rewarded us according to our iniquities. For as the heaven is high above the earth, so great is His mercy toward them that fear Him. As far as the east is from the west, so far has He removed our transgressions from us.
PSALM 103:10–12

The LORD will perfect that which concerns me: Your mercy, O LORD, endures for ever: forsake not the works of Your own hands.   PSALM 138:8

Let the wicked forsake his way, and the unrighteous man his thoughts: and let him return to the LORD, and He will have mercy upon him; and to our God, for He will abundantly pardon.
ISAIAH 55:7

For God sent not His Son into the world to condemn the world; but that the world through Him might be saved.   JOHN 3:17

Jesus says to him, Rise, take up your bed, and walk.   JOHN 5:8

And God is able to make all grace abound toward you; that you, always having all sufficiency in all things, may abound to every good work.   2 CORINTHIANS 9:8

And He said to me, My grace is sufficient for you: for My strength is made perfect in weakness. Most gladly therefore will I rather glory in my infirmities, that the power of Christ may rest upon me.   2 CORINTHIANS 12:9

But God commends His love toward us, in that, while we were yet sinners, Christ died for us.   ROMANS 5:8

There is therefore now no condemnation to them which are in Christ Jesus, who walk not after the flesh, but after the Spirit.
ROMANS 8:1

Grace and peace be multiplied to you through the knowledge of God, and of Jesus our Lord, According as His divine power has given to us all things that pertain to life and godliness, through the knowledge of Him that has called us to glory and virtue.
2 PETER 1:2–3

Grace be with you, mercy, and peace, from God the Father, and from the Lord Jesus Christ, the Son of the Father, in truth and love.   2 JOHN 3

INSIGHTS ON FAITH FROM SMITH WIGGLESWORTH

His Word has a life-giving power. The psalmist knew it; he said that God's Word had given him life (Ps. 119:50). This Word is the divine revelation; it is the Word of life, of healing, of power. God has given us His own Word. I wish that all who can hear me would give themselves over to carefully reading more of the Word of God.

How can we describe this faith? It is genuine and pure. It never wavers. It is confident and sensitive to the breath of God. This faith, which is the very nature of the Son of God, comes from the Author of faith. It is holy in action, dares to believe, rests assured, and sees the mighty power of God evidenced in its workings. It is a living faith that allows us to claim all that He has for us. Faith sees *"the crooked places… made straight"* (Isa. 40:4). It sees *"the lame…leap like a deer"* (Isa. 35:6). It is not surprised when *"the blind see"* (Matt. 11:5). God has finished creation; it is forever completed by the perfect work of our Lord. We are *"complete in Him, who is the head of all principality and power"* (Col. 2:10). We are His righteousness and created for His purpose.

FOR GOD'S FAVOR

God be merciful to us, and bless us; and cause His face to shine upon us; Selah. That Your way may be known upon earth, Your saving health among all nations. PSALM 67:1–2

Remember me, O LORD, with the favor that You bear to Your people: O visit me with Your salvation. PSALM 106:4

No weapon that is formed against you shall prosper; and every tongue that shall rise against you in judgment you shall condemn. This is the heritage of the servants of the LORD, and their righteousness is of Me, says the LORD. ISAIAH 54:17

Above all, taking the shield of faith, wherewith you shall be able to quench all the fiery darts of the wicked. And take the helmet of salvation, and the sword of the Spirit, which is the word of God. EPHESIANS 6:16–17

You are of God, little children, and have overcome them: because greater is He that is in you, than he that is in the world. 1 JOHN 4:4

FOR GUIDANCE

And the Lord went before them by day in a pillar of a cloud, to lead them the way; and by night in a pillar of fire, to give them light; to go by day and night: He took not away the pillar of the cloud by day, nor the pillar of fire by night, from before the people.   Exodus 13:21–22

Show me Your ways, O Lord; teach me Your paths. Lead me in Your truth, and teach me: for You are the God of my salvation; on You do I wait all the day.   Psalm 25:4–5

The steps of a good man are ordered by the Lord: and He delights in his way.   Psalm 37:23

For this God is our God for ever and ever: He will be our guide even to death.   Psalm 48:14

You through Your commandments have made me wiser than my enemies: for they are ever with me.   Psalm 119:98

You compass my path and my lying down, and are acquainted with all my ways.   Psalm 139:3

For the Lord gives wisdom: out of His mouth comes knowledge and understanding.   Proverbs 2:6

When you go, it shall lead you; when you sleep, it shall keep you; and when you awake, it shall talk with you. For the commandment is a lamp; and the law is light; and reproofs of instruction are the way of life. PROVERBS 6:22–23

The way of a fool is right in his own eyes: but he that hearkens to counsel is wise. PROVERBS 12:15

Commit your works to the LORD, and your thoughts shall be established. PROVERBS 16:3

Then shall we know, if we follow on to know the LORD: His going forth is prepared as the morning; and He shall come to us as the rain, as the latter and former rain to the earth. HOSEA 6:3

Jesus answered and said to him, If a man love Me, he will keep My words: and My Father will love him, and We will come to him, and make Our abode with him. He that loves Me not keeps not My sayings: and the word which you hear is not Mine, but the Father's which sent Me. JOHN 14:23–24

If any of you lack wisdom, let him ask of God, that gives to all men liberally, and upbraids not; and it shall be given him. JAMES 1:5

INSIGHTS ON FAITH FROM SMITH WIGGLESWORTH

In every way that the Word of God speaks to you, faith lends its help. Faith stirs you. Faith says to you, "If you believe, you will receive. If you dare to believe, oneness, purity, power, and eternal fact are working through you."

⌣

Step into the full tide of the life of the manifestation of God. Your new nature has no corruption in it. Eternal life is not just during your lifetime; it is forever. You are regenerated by the power of the Word of God, and it is in you as an incorruptible force, taking you on from victory to victory until death itself can be overcome, until sin has no authority, until disease could not be in the body. This is a living fact by the Word of God.

⌣

God wants us to be powerful, a people of faith, a purified people, a people who will launch out in God and dare to trust Him in glorious faith, which always takes you beyond what is commonplace to an abiding place in God.

FOR HEALING

And, behold, I am with you, and will keep you in all places wherever you go, and will bring you again into this land; for I will not leave you, until I have done that which I have spoken to you of.
GENESIS 28:15

And He has put a new song in my mouth, even praise to our God: many shall see it, and fear, and shall trust in the LORD.
PSALM 40:3

He heals the broken in heart, and binds up their wounds.
PSALM 147:3

It shall be health to your navel, and marrow to your bones.
PROVERBS 3:8

And it shall come to pass in that day, that his burden shall be taken away from off your shoulder, and his yoke from off your neck, and the yoke shall be destroyed because of the anointing.
ISAIAH 10:27

He gives power to the faint; and to them that have no might He increases strength. Even the youths shall faint and be weary, and the young men shall utterly fall: but they that wait upon the LORD shall renew their strength; they shall mount up with wings as eagles; they shall run, and not be weary; and they shall walk, and not faint.
ISAIAH 40:29–31

But He was wounded for our transgressions, He was bruised for our iniquities: the chastisement of our peace was upon Him; and with His stripes we are healed.　　　　Isaiah 53:5

Behold, I will bring it health and cure, and I will cure them, and will reveal to them the abundance of peace and truth.

Jeremiah 33:6

That it might be fulfilled which was spoken by Isaiah the prophet, saying, Himself took our infirmities, and bore our sicknesses.

Matthew 8:17

And Jesus went about all the cities and villages, teaching in their synagogues, and preaching the gospel of the kingdom, and healing every sickness and every disease among the people.

Matthew 9:35

Come to Me, all you that labor and are heavy laden, and I will give you rest.　　　　Matthew 11:28

For we have not an high priest which cannot be touched with the feeling of our infirmities; but was in all points tempted like as we are, yet without sin.　　　　Hebrews 4:15

Is any among you afflicted? let him pray. Is any merry? let him sing psalms. Is any sick among you? let him call for the elders of the church; and let them pray over him, anointing him with oil in the name of the Lord: and the prayer of faith shall save the sick, and the Lord shall raise him up; and if he have committed sins, they shall be forgiven him. Confess your faults one to another, and pray one for another, that you may be healed. The effectual fervent prayer of a righteous man avails much. JAMES 5:13–16

Forasmuch as you know that you were not redeemed with corruptible things, as silver and gold, from your vain conversation received by tradition from your fathers; but with the precious blood of Christ, as of a lamb without blemish and without spot: who verily was foreordained before the foundation of the world, but was manifest in these last times for you, who by Him do believe in God, that raised Him up from the dead, and gave Him glory; that your faith and hope might be in God.

1 PETER 1:18–21

God shall wipe away all tears from their eyes; and there shall be no more death, neither sorrow, nor crying, neither shall there be any more pain: for the former things are passed away.

REVELATION 21:4

INSIGHTS ON FAITH FROM SMITH WIGGLESWORTH

Everyone who has desires for God should believe the Word of God and take Jesus as the Author and the Finisher of his faith. All the desires and purposes of your heart will be accomplished, because God is faithful. God cannot fail; His Word is true.

⌐⌐

God is making manifest His power. God is a reality and is proving His mightiness in the midst of us. And as we open ourselves to divine revelation and get rid of all things that are not of the Spirit, then we will understand how mightily God can take us on in the Spirit, move the things that appear, and bring the things that do not appear into prominence.

⌐⌐

The most trying time is the most helpful time. Most preachers say something about Daniel and about the Hebrew children, Shadrach, Meshach, and Abednego, and especially about Moses when he was tried and in a corner. Beloved, if you read the Scriptures, you will never find anything about the easy times. All the glories came out of hard times.

"WE MUST NEVER THINK ABOUT OUR GOD IN SMALL WAYS. HE SPOKE THE WORD ONE DAY AND MADE THE WORLD. THAT IS THE KIND OF GOD WE HAVE, AND HE IS JUST THE SAME TODAY. THERE IS NO CHANGE IN HIM. OH, HE IS LOVELY AND PRECIOUS ABOVE ALL THOUGHT AND COMPARISON. THERE IS NONE LIKE HIM."

—SMITH WIGGLESWORTH

2

THE LIVING POWER OF FAITH TO...

OVERCOME ANGER

Cease from anger, and forsake wrath: fret not yourself in any wise to do evil. PSALM 37:8

He that is slow to anger is better than the mighty; and he that rules his spirit than he that takes a city. PROVERBS 16:32

The discretion of a man defers his anger; and it is his glory to pass over a transgression. PROVERBS 19:11

But I say to you, That whosoever is angry with his brother without a cause shall be in danger of the judgment: and whosoever shall say to his brother, Raca, shall be in danger of the council: but whosoever shall say, You fool, shall be in danger of hell fire. MATTHEW 5:22

RELIEVE ANXIETY

Have not I commanded you? Be strong and of a good courage; be not afraid, neither be you dismayed: for the L ORD *your God is with you wherever you go.*   J OSHUA 1:9

They that trust in the L ORD *shall be as mount Zion, which cannot be removed, but abides for ever.*   P SALM 125:1

And why take you thought for raiment? Consider the lilies of the field, how they grow; they toil not, neither do they spin: and yet I say to you, that even Solomon in all his glory was not arrayed like one of these. Wherefore, if God so clothe the grass of the field, which to day is, and tomorrow is cast into the oven, shall He not much more clothe you, O you of little faith?

M ATTHEW 6:28–30

And He said to His disciples, Therefore I say to you, Take no thought for your life, what you shall eat; neither for the body, what you shall put on. The life is more than meat, and the body is more than raiment.   L UKE 12:22–23

Then said Jesus to those Jews which believed on Him, If you continue in My word, then are you My disciples indeed; and you shall know the truth, and the truth shall make you free.

J OHN 8:31–32

Be careful for nothing; but in every thing by prayer and supplication with thanksgiving let your requests be made known to God. And the peace of God, which passes all understanding, shall keep your hearts and minds through Christ Jesus. Finally, brethren, whatsoever things are true, whatsoever things are honest, whatsoever things are just, whatsoever things are pure, whatsoever things are lovely, whatsoever things are of good report; if there be any virtue, and if there be any praise, think on these things.

PHILIPPIANS 4:6–8

Nay, in all these things we are more than conquerors through Him that loved us. ROMANS 8:37

Let no man deceive you by any means: for that day shall not come, except there come a falling away first, and that man of sin be revealed, the son of perdition. 2 THESSALONIANS 2:3

Who are kept by the power of God through faith to salvation ready to be revealed in the last time. 1 PETER 1:5

INSIGHTS ON FAITH FROM SMITH WIGGLESWORTH

It is when you are tried by fire that God purges you, takes the dross away, and brings forth the pure gold. Only melted gold is minted. Only soft wax receives the seal. Only broken, contrite hearts receive the mark as the Potter turns us on His wheel, shaped and burned to take and keep the heavenly mold, the stamp of God's pure gold.

ᘛᘛ

I understand God by His Word. I cannot understand God by impressions or feelings. I cannot get to know God by sentiments. If I am going to know God, I am going to know Him by His Word. I know I will be in heaven, but I cannot determine from my feelings that I am going to heaven. I am going to heaven because God's Word says it, and I believe God's Word. And "*faith comes by hearing, and hearing by the word of God*" (Rom. 10:17).

ᘛᘛ

Faith is always accompanied by peace. Faith always rests. Faith laughs at impossibilities. Salvation is by faith, through grace, and "*it is the gift of God*" (Eph. 2:8).

DEFEAT DEPRESSION

The eternal God is your refuge, and underneath are the everlasting arms: and He shall thrust out the enemy from before you; and shall say, Destroy them. DEUTERONOMY 33:27

For you are my lamp, O LORD: and the LORD will lighten my darkness. 2 SAMUEL 22:29

Then he said unto them, Go your way, eat the fat, and drink the sweet, and send portions to them for whom nothing is prepared: for this day is holy to our LORD: neither be you sorry; for the joy of the LORD is your strength. NEHEMIAH 8:10

For I said in my haste, I am cut off from before Your eyes: nevertheless You heard the voice of my supplications when I cried to You. O love the LORD, all you His saints: for the LORD preserves the faithful, and plentifully rewards the proud doer. Be of good courage, and He shall strengthen your heart, all you that hope in the LORD. PSALM 31:22–24

I sought the LORD, and He heard me, and delivered me from all my fears. PSALM 34:4

Many are the afflictions of the righteous: but the LORD delivers him out of them all. PSALM 34:19

The steps of a good man are ordered by the Lord: *and He delights in his way. Though he fall, he shall not be utterly cast down: for the* Lord *upholds him with His hand.*   Psalm 37:23–24

God is our refuge and strength, a very present help in trouble. Therefore will not we fear, though the earth be removed, and though the mountains be carried into the midst of the sea; though the waters thereof roar and be troubled, though the mountains shake with the swelling thereof.   Psalm 46:1–3

For Your lovingkindness is before my eyes: and I have walked in Your truth.   Psalm 26:3

When you pass through the waters, I will be with you; and through the rivers, they shall not overflow you: when you walk through the fire, you shall not be burned; neither shall the flame kindle upon you.   Isaiah 43:2

For the Lord *will not cast off for ever: but though He cause grief, yet will He have compassion according to the multitude of His mercies.*   Lamentations 3:31–32

Let not your heart be troubled: you believe in God, believe also in Me.   John 14:1

We are troubled on every side, yet not distressed; we are perplexed, but not in despair; persecuted, but not forsaken; cast down, but not destroyed.   2 Corinthians 4:8–9

INSIGHTS ON FAITH FROM SMITH WIGGLESWORTH

When you stand in faith, you are in a position in which God can take you to the place where you are *"over all"* (Luke 10:19) by the power of God.

⌒

Believe that no power of the Enemy will have power over you. Rebuke him. Stand on the authority of the Word and go forth into victory. I want you to be saved, healed, and blessed through what God's Word says.

⌒

What an inheritance is ours when the very nature, the very righteousness, the very power of the Father and the Son are made real in us. This is God's purpose, and as by faith, we take hold of the purpose, we will always be conscious that *"He who is in* [us] *is greater than he who is in the world"* (1 John 4:4). The purpose of all Scripture is to move us to this wonderful and blessed elevation of faith where our constant experience is the manifestation of God's life and power through us.

CONQUER DOUBT

They shall not hunger nor thirst; neither shall the heat nor sun smite them: for He that has mercy on them shall lead them, even by the springs of water shall He guide them.   ISAIAH 49:10

Truly my soul waits upon God: from Him comes my salvation. He only is my rock and my salvation; He is my defence; I shall not be greatly moved.   PSALM 62:1–2

My flesh and my heart fails: but God is the strength of my heart, and my portion for ever.   PSALM 73:26

When I said, my foot slips; Your mercy, O LORD, held me up. In the multitude of my thoughts within me Your comforts delight my soul.   PSALM 94:18–19

And immediately Jesus stretched forth His hand, and caught him, and said to him, O you of little faith, wherefore did you doubt?
      MATTHEW 14:31

But whosoever drinks of the water that I shall give him shall never thirst; but the water that I shall give him shall be in him a well of water springing up into everlasting life.   JOHN 4:14

HELP DURING TROUBLE

The LORD also will be a refuge for the oppressed, a refuge in times of trouble.   PSALM 9:9

The LORD is my rock, and my fortress, and my deliverer; my God, my strength, in whom I will trust; my buckler, and the horn of my salvation, and my high tower.   PSALM 18:2

For You will light my candle: the LORD my God will enlighten my darkness.   PSALM 18:28

For He has not despised nor abhorred the affliction of the afflicted; neither has He hid His face from him; but when he cried to Him, He heard.   PSALM 22:24

Lead me in Your truth, and teach me: for You are the God of my salvation; on You do I wait all the day.   PSALM 25:5

The LORD is my strength and my shield; my heart trusted in Him, and I am helped: therefore my heart greatly rejoices; and with my song will I praise Him.   PSALM 28:7

O love the LORD, all you His saints: for the LORD preserves the faithful.   PSALM 31:23

You are my hiding place; You shall preserve me from trouble; You shall compass me about with songs of deliverance.   PSALM 32:7

But the salvation of the righteous is of the LORD: He is their strength in the time of trouble.   PSALM 37:39

Cast your burden upon the LORD, and He shall sustain you: He shall never allow the righteous to be moved.   PSALM 55:22

There shall no evil befall you, neither shall any plague come near your dwelling. For He shall give His angels charge over you, to keep you in all your ways.   PSALM 91:10–11

The LORD opens the eyes of the blind: the LORD raises them that are bowed down: the LORD loves the righteous.   PSALM 146:8

Dearly beloved, avenge not yourselves, but rather give place to wrath: for it is written, Vengeance is Mine; I will repay, says the Lord. Therefore if your enemy hunger, feed him; if he thirst, give him drink: for in so doing you shall heap coals of fire on his head. Be not overcome of evil, but overcome evil with good.

ROMANS 12:19–21

INSIGHTS ON FAITH FROM SMITH WIGGLESWORTH

Everything depends upon our believing God. If we are saved, it is only because God's Word says so. We cannot rest upon our feelings. We cannot do anything without a living faith.

⌒

"Faith is the substance of things hoped for" (Heb. 11:1). I want to speak about *"substance"*; it is a remarkable word. Many people come to me and say, "I want things to be tangible. I want something to appeal to my human reasoning." My response to this is that everything that you cannot see is eternal. Everything you can see is natural and fades away. Everything you see now will fade away and will be consumed, but what you cannot see, what is more real than you, is the substance of all things: God in the human soul, mightier than you by a million times.

⌒

God will not fail His Word, whatever you are. Suppose that all the people in the world did not believe; that would make no difference to God's Word; it would be the same. You cannot alter God's Word. It is from everlasting to everlasting, and they who believe in it will be like Mount Zion, which cannot be moved.

ACTIVATE FAITH

And he believed in the Lord; *and He counted it to him for righteousness.* Genesis 15:6

Trust in the Lord *with all your heart; and lean not to your own understanding.* Proverbs 3:5

Behold, his soul which is lifted up is not upright in him: but the just shall live by his faith. Habakkuk 2:4

Whosoever therefore shall break one of these least commandments, and shall teach men so, he shall be called the least in the kingdom of heaven: but whosoever shall do and teach them, the same shall be called great in the kingdom of heaven.

Matthew 5:19

For with God nothing shall be impossible. Luke 1:37

And the apostles said to the Lord, Increase our faith. And the Lord said, If you had faith as a grain of mustard seed, you might say to this sycamine tree, Be you plucked up by the root, and be you planted in the sea; and it should obey you. Luke 17:5–6

And He said, The things which are impossible with men are possible with God. Luke 18:27

Confirming the souls of the disciples, and exhorting them to continue in the faith, and that we must through much tribulation enter into the kingdom of God. ACTS 14:22

And now why tarriest you? Arise, and be baptized, and wash away your sins, calling on the name of the Lord. ACTS 22:16

But the fruit of the Spirit is love, joy, peace, longsuffering, gentleness, goodness, faith, meekness, temperance: against such there is no law. GALATIANS 5:22–23

We give thanks to God and the Father of our Lord Jesus Christ, praying always for you, since we heard of your faith in Christ Jesus, and of the love which you have to all the saints, for the hope which is laid up for you in heaven, whereof you heard before in the word of the truth of the gospel. COLOSSIANS 1:3–5

Now the just shall live by faith: but if any man draw back, My soul shall have no pleasure in him. But we are not of them who draw back to perdition; but of them that believe to the saving of the soul. HEBREWS 10:38–39

If any of you lack wisdom, let him ask of God, that gives to all men liberally, and upbraids not; and it shall be given him. But let him ask in faith, nothing wavering. For he that wavers is like a wave of the sea driven with the wind and tossed. For let not that man think that he shall receive any thing of the Lord. A double minded man is unstable in all his ways.   JAMES 1:5–8

Even so faith, if it has not works, is dead, being alone. Yea, a man may say, You have faith, and I have works: show me your faith without your works, and I will show you my faith by my works. You believe that there is one God; you do well: the devils also believe, and tremble.   JAMES 2:17–19

You see then how that by works a man is justified, and not by faith only.   JAMES 2:24

For as the body without the spirit is dead, so faith without works is dead also.   JAMES 2:26

Whosoever transgresses, and abides not in the doctrine of Christ, has not God. He that abides in the doctrine of Christ, he has both the Father and the Son.   2 JOHN 1:9

INSIGHTS ON FAITH FROM SMITH WIGGLESWORTH

Jesus is the Word, and if you have the Word, you have faith: "like…faith."

⌒

There are two kinds of faith that God wants to let us see. I am not speaking about natural things but divine things. There is a natural faith, and there is a saving faith. The saving faith is the gift of God. All people are born with the natural faith. But this supernatural faith is the gift of God. Yet there are limitations in this faith. Faith that has no limitation in God can be seen in the twenty-sixth chapter of Acts.

⌒

If you believe in your heart, you can begin to speak, and whatever you say will come to pass if you believe in your heart. Ask God to give you the grace to use the faith you have.

RECEIVE GOD'S LOVE

And it shall come to pass, if you shall hearken diligently unto my commandments which I command you this day, to love the Lord *your God, and to serve Him with all your heart and with all your soul, that I will give you the rain of your land in his due season, the first rain and the latter rain, that you may gather in your corn, and your wine, and your oil. And I will send grass in your fields for your cattle, that you may eat and be full.*

Deuteronomy 11:13–15

And the Lord*, He it is that does go before you; He will be with you, He will not fail you, neither forsake you: fear not, neither be dismayed.*

Deuteronomy 31:8

I have called upon You, for You will hear me, O God: incline Your ear to me, and hear my speech. Show your marvelous lovingkindness, O You that save by Your right hand them which put their trust in You from those that rise up against them. Keep me as the apple of the eye, hide me under the shadow of Your wings, From the wicked that oppress me, from my deadly enemies, who compass me about.

Psalm 17:6–9

The Lord *will give strength to His people; the* Lord *will bless His people with peace.*

Psalm 29:11

I sought the LORD, and He heard me, and delivered me from all my fears. They looked to Him, and were lightened: and their faces were not ashamed.   PSALM 34:4–5

Why are you cast down, O my soul? and why are you disquieted within me? hope you in God: for I shall yet praise Him, who is the health of my countenance, and my God.   PSALM 42:11

I will abundantly bless her provision: I will satisfy her poor with bread.   PSALM 132:15

The way of the wicked is an abomination to the LORD: but He loves him that follows after righteousness.   PROVERBS 15:9

Yea, I will rejoice over them to do them good, and I will plant them in this land assuredly with My whole heart and with My whole soul.   JEREMIAH 32:41

And I will make them and the places round about My hill a blessing; and I will cause the shower to come down in his season; there shall be showers of blessing.   EZEKIEL 34:26

Come to Me, all you that labor and are heavy laden, and I will give you rest.   MATTHEW 11:28

For the Father Himself loves you, because you have loved Me, and have believed that I came out from God.   JOHN 16:27

For God so loved the world, that He gave His only begotten Son, that whosoever believes in Him should not perish, but have everlasting life.   JOHN 3:16

But as it is written, Eye has not seen, nor ear heard, neither have entered into the heart of man, the things which God has prepared for them that love Him.   1 CORINTHIANS 2:9

But God, who is rich in mercy, for His great love wherewith He loved us, even when we were dead in sins, has quickened us together with Christ, by grace you are saved. And has raised us up together, and made us sit together in heavenly places in Christ Jesus.   EPHESIANS 2:4–6

In this was manifested the love of God toward us, because that God sent His only begotten Son into the world, that we might live through Him. Herein is love, not that we loved God, but that He loved us, and sent His Son to be the propitiation for our sins. Beloved, if God so loved us, we ought also to love one another.

1 JOHN 4:9–11

INSIGHTS ON FAITH FROM SMITH WIGGLESWORTH

"He who believes." What a word! God's Word changes us, and we enter into fellowship and communion. We enter into assurance and Godlikeness, for we see the truth and believe. Faith is an effective power; God opens the understanding and reveals Himself. *"Therefore it is of faith that it might be according to grace"* (Rom. 4:16). Grace is God's blessing coming down to you. You open the door to God as an act of faith, and God does all you want.

⌒

The Bible is the Word of God. It has the truths, and whatever people may say of them, they stand stationary, unmovable. Not one word of all His good promises will fail. His Word will come forth. In heaven it is settled (Ps. 119:89). On earth the fact must be made manifest that He is the God of everlasting power.

PRAY EXPECTANTLY

If My people, which are called by My name, shall humble themselves, and pray, and seek My face, and turn from their wicked ways; then will I hear from heaven, and will forgive their sin, and will heal their land.   2 CHRONICLES 7:14

For the people shall dwell in Zion at Jerusalem: you shall weep no more: He will be very gracious to you at the voice of your cry; when He shall hear it, He will answer you.   ISAIAH 30:19

And it shall come to pass, that before they call, I will answer; and while they are yet speaking, I will hear.   ISAIAH 65:24

And I will bring the third part through the fire, and will refine them as silver is refined, and will try them as gold is tried: they shall call on My name, and I will hear them: I will say, It is My people: and they shall say, The LORD is my God.

ZECHARIAH 13:9

But you, when you pray, enter into your closet, and when you have shut thy door, pray to your Father which is in secret; and your Father which sees in secret shall reward you openly.

MATTHEW 6:6

After this manner therefore pray you: Our Father which is in heaven, hallowed be Your name. Your kingdom come, Your will be done in earth, as it is in heaven. Give us this day our daily bread. And forgive us our debts, as we forgive our debtors. And lead us not into temptation, but deliver us from evil: for Yours is the kingdom, and the power, and the glory, for ever. Amen.

MATTHEW 6:9–13

Ask, and it shall be given you; seek, and you shall find; knock, and it shall be opened to you: for every one that asks receives; and he that seeks finds; and to him that knocks it shall be opened.

MATTHEW 7:7–8

If you then, being evil, know how to give good gifts to your children, how much more shall your Father which is in heaven give good things to them that ask Him?   MATTHEW 7:11

And all things, whatsoever you shall ask in prayer, believing, you shall receive.   MATTHEW 21:22

And whatsoever you shall ask in My name, that will I do, that the Father may be glorified in the Son. If you shall ask any thing in My name, I will do it.   JOHN 14:13–14

If you abide in Me, and My words abide in you, you shall ask what you will, and it shall be done to you.   JOHN 15:7

And in that day you shall ask Me nothing. Verily, verily, I say to you, Whatsoever you shall ask the Father in My name, He will give it you. Until now have you asked nothing in My name: ask, and you shall receive, that your joy may be full.

JOHN 16:23–24

Praying always with all prayer and supplication in the Spirit, and watching thereto with all perseverance and supplication for all saints. EPHESIANS 6:18

Pray without ceasing. 1 THESSALONIANS 5:17

Confess your faults one to another, and pray one for another, that ye may be healed. The effectual fervent prayer of a righteous man avails much. JAMES 5:16

And this is the confidence that we have in Him, that, if we ask any thing according to His will, He hears us: and if we know that He hear us, whatsoever we ask, we know that we have the petitions that we desired of Him. 1 JOHN 5:14–15

INSIGHTS ON FAITH FROM SMITH WIGGLESWORTH

Faith is just the open door through which the Lord comes. Do not say, "I was saved by faith" or "I was healed by faith." Faith does not save and heal. God saves and heals through that open door. You believe, and the power of Christ comes. Salvation and healing are for the glory of God.

⌒

It is one thing to handle the Word of God, but it is another thing to believe what God says. The great aim of the Spirit's power within us is to so bring us in line with His perfect will that we will unhesitatingly believe the Scriptures, daring to accept them as the authentic, divine principle of God. When we do, we will find our feet so firmly fixed upon the plan of redemption that it will not matter where our trials or other things come from, for our whole natures will be so enlarged that we will no longer focus on ourselves but will say, "Lord, what do You want me to do?"

VANQUISH PRIDE

And whatsoever my eyes desired I kept not from them, I withheld not my heart from any joy; for my heart rejoiced in all my labor: and this was my portion of all my labor. Then I looked on all the works that my hands had wrought, and on the labor that I had labored to do: and, behold, all was vanity and vexation of spirit, and there was no profit under the sun. ECCLESIASTES 2:10–11

Even the youths shall faint and be weary, and the young men shall utterly fall: but they that wait upon the LORD *shall renew their strength; they shall mount up with wings as eagles; they shall run, and not be weary; and they shall walk, and not faint.*

ISAIAH 40:30–31

Now therefore thus says the LORD *of hosts; Consider your ways.*

HAGGAI 1:5

We then that are strong ought to bear the infirmities of the weak, and not to please ourselves. Let every one of us please his neighbor for his good to edification. ROMANS 15:1–2

Look not every man on his own things, but every man also on the things of others. Let this mind be in you, which was also in Christ Jesus. PHILIPPIANS 2:4–5

ABOLISH WORRY

There shall not any man be able to stand before you all the days of your life: as I was with Moses, so I will be with you: I will not fail you, nor forsake you.   JOSHUA 1:5

If you would seek to God betimes, and make your supplication to the Almighty; if you were pure and upright; surely now He would awake for you, and make the habitation of your righteousness prosperous.   JOB 8:5–6

The angel of the LORD encamps round about them that fear Him, and delivers them.   PSALM 34:7

Many are the afflictions of the righteous: but the LORD delivers him out of them all.   PSALM 34:19

My eyes shall be upon the faithful of the land, that they may dwell with Me: he that walks in a perfect way, he shall serve Me.
                              PSALM 101:6

Take counsel together, and it shall come to nothing; speak the word, and it shall not stand: for God is with us.   ISAIAH 8:10

If you then, being evil, know how to give good gifts to your children, how much more shall your Father which is in heaven give good things to them that ask Him?   MATTHEW 7:11

Be careful for nothing; but in every thing by prayer and supplication with thanksgiving let your requests be made known to God. And the peace of God, which passes all understanding, shall keep your hearts and minds through Christ Jesus.

PHILIPPIANS 4:6–7

I can do all things through Christ which strengthens me.

PHILIPPIANS 4:13

Let your conversation be without covetousness; and be content with such things as you have: for He has said, I will never leave you, nor forsake you.　　　　HEBREWS 13:5

For God has not given us the spirit of fear; but of power, and of love, and of a sound mind.　　　　2 TIMOTHY 1:7

You are of God, little children, and have overcome them: because greater is He that is in you, than he that is in the world.

1 JOHN 4:4

INSIGHTS ON FAITH FROM SMITH WIGGLESWORTH

When you have the right attitude, your faith becomes remarkably active. Faith cannot be remarkably active in a dead life; it is active only when your sins have been forgiven, your body is clean, and your life is made right. When these things are true, the Holy Ghost comes, and faith is the evidence.

Everyone who asks receives. He who is asking is receiving. He who is seeking is finding. The door has been opened right now; that is, God's present Word. The verse does not say, "Ask and ye shall not receive." Believe that asking is receiving, seeking is finding, and to him who is knocking, the door is being opened.

God wants us to move mountains. Anything that appears to be like a mountain can be moved: the mountains of difficulty, the mountains of perplexity, the mountains of depression or depravity—things that have bound you for years. Sometimes things appear as though they could not be moved, but you can believe in your heart and stand on the Word of God, and God's Word will never be defeated.

"GOD BLESS YOU! WHEN HE BLESSES, NO ONE CAN CURSE. WHEN GOD IS WITH YOU, IT IS IMPOSSIBLE FOR ANYONE TO BE AGAINST YOU. WHEN GOD HAS PUT HIS HAND UPON YOU, EVERY WAY WILL OPEN WITH BENEDICTION TO OTHERS. THE GREATEST THING THAT GOD HAS ALLOWED US TO COME INTO IS THE PLAN OF DISTRIBUTING HIS BLESSING TO OTHERS. 'I WILL BLESS THEE...AND THOU SHALT BE A BLESSING.'"

—SMITH WIGGLESWORTH

3

DARE TO BELIEVE

BELIEF IN JESUS

Jesus said to the centurion, Go your way; and as you have believed, so be it done to you. And his servant was healed in the selfsame hour.   MATTHEW 8:13

And when He was come into the house, the blind men came to Him: and Jesus says to them, Believe you that I am able to do this? They said to Him, Yea, Lord.   MATTHEW 9:28

And Jesus said to them, I am the bread of life: he that comes to Me shall never hunger; and he that believes on Me shall never thirst.
                                                    JOHN 6:35

I am come a light into the world, that whosoever believes on Me should not abide in darkness.   JOHN 12:46

Let not your heart be troubled: you believe in God, believe also in Me. JOHN 14:1

Jesus says to him, I am the way, the truth, and the life: no man comes to the Father, but by Me. JOHN 14:6

To Him give all the prophets witness, that through His name whosoever believes in Him shall receive remission of sins.

ACTS 10:43

How then shall they call on Him in whom they have not believed? and how shall they believe in Him of whom they have not heard? and how shall they hear without a preacher? and how shall they preach, except they be sent? as it is written, How beautiful are the feet of them that preach the gospel of peace, and bring glad tidings of good things! ROMANS 10:14–15

Wherefore also it is contained in the scripture, Behold, I lay in Zion a chief corner stone, elect, precious: and he that believes on Him shall not be confounded. 1 PETER 2:6

Hereby know you the Spirit of God: Every spirit that confesses that Jesus Christ is come in the flesh is of God. 1 JOHN 4:2

BLESSINGS

And Jabez called on the God of Israel, saying, Oh that You would bless me indeed, and enlarge my coast, and that Your hand might be with me, and that You would keep me from evil, that it may not grieve me! And God granted him that which he requested.

1 CHRONICLES 4:10

Arise, O LORD, disappoint him, cast him down: deliver my soul from the wicked, which is Your sword: from men which are Your hand, O LORD, from men of the world, which have their portion in this life, and whose belly you fill with Your hid treasure: they are full of children, and leave the rest of their substance to their babes.

PSALM 17:13–14

I will sing of the mercies of the LORD for ever: with my mouth will I make known Your faithfulness to all generations. For I have said, Mercy shall be built up for ever: Your faithfulness shall You establish in the very heavens.

PSALM 89:1–2

Blessed is the man whom You chasten, O LORD, and teach him out of Your law; that You may give him rest from the days of adversity, until the pit be dug for the wicked.   PSALM 94:12–13

He that walks righteously, and speaks uprightly; he that despises the gain of oppressions, that shakes his hands from holding of bribes, that stops his ears from hearing of blood, and shuts his eyes from seeing evil; he shall dwell on high: his place of defence shall be the munitions of rocks: bread shall be given him; his waters shall be sure. ISAIAH 33:15–16

The LORD has been mindful of us: He will bless us; He will bless the house of Israel; He will bless the house of Aaron. He will bless them that fear the LORD, both small and great. The LORD shall increase you more and more, you and your children. PSALM 115:12–14

Follow peace with all men, and holiness, without which no man shall see the Lord. HEBREWS 12:14

But the wisdom that is from above is first pure, then peaceable, gentle, and easy to be entreated, full of mercy and good fruits, without partiality, and without hypocrisy. JAMES 3:17

For he that will love life, and see good days, let him refrain his tongue from evil, and his lips that they speak no guile: let him eschew evil, and do good; let him seek peace, and ensue it. 1 PETER 3:10–11

INSIGHTS ON FAITH FROM SMITH WIGGLESWORTH

Yes, "*faith is the substance of things hoped for, the evidence of things not seen*" (Heb. 11:1). Faith is what came into me when I believed. I was born of the incorruptible Word by the living virtue, life, and personality of God. I was instantly changed from nature to grace. I became a servant of God, and I became an enemy of unrighteousness.

⌒

Faith in God and power with God lie in the knowledge of the Word of God. We are no better than our faith. "*For whatever is born of God overcomes the world. And this is the victory that has overcome the world; our faith*" (1 John 5:4). If you believe in Him, you are purified, for He is pure. You are strengthened, for He is strong. You are made whole, because He is whole.

⌒

You will never go through with God in any area except by believing Him. It is "Thus says the Lord" every time, and you will see the plan of God come right through when you dare to believe.

CORRECTION

You shall also consider in your heart, that, as a man chastens his son, so the LORD your God chastens you. Therefore you shall keep the commandments of the LORD your God, to walk in His ways, and to fear Him.   DEUTERONOMY 8:5–6

For whom the LORD loves He corrects; even as a father the son in whom he delights.   PROVERBS 3:12

For all things are for your sakes, that the abundant grace might through the thanksgiving of many redound to the glory of God. For which cause we faint not; but though our outward man perish, yet the inward man is renewed day by day.
2 CORINTHIANS 4:15–16

For whom the Lord loves He chastens, and scourges every son whom He receives. If you endure chastening, God deals with you as with sons; for what son is he whom the father chastens not?
HEBREWS 12:6–7

For they verily for a few days chastened us after their own pleasure; but He for our profit, that we might be partakers of His holiness. Now no chastening for the present seems to be joyous, but grievous: nevertheless afterward it yields the peaceable fruit of righteousness to them which are exercised thereby.
HEBREWS 12:10–11

DESERT PLACES

Yet You in Your manifold mercies forsook them not in the wilderness: the pillar of the cloud departed not from them by day, to lead them in the way; neither the pillar of fire by night, to show them light, and the way wherein they should go. You gave also Your good Spirit to instruct them, and withheld not Your manna from their mouth, and gave them water for their thirst. Yea, forty years did You sustain them in the wilderness, so that they lacked nothing; their clothes waxed not old, and their feet swelled not.

NEHEMIAH 9:19–21

I will open rivers in high places, and fountains in the midst of the valleys: I will make the wilderness a pool of water, and the dry land springs of water.

ISAIAH 41:18

Jesus answered and said to her, Whosoever drinks of this water shall thirst again: but whosoever drinks of the water that I shall give him shall never thirst; but the water that I shall give him shall be in him a well of water springing up into everlasting life.

JOHN 4:13–14

He that believes on Me, as the scripture has said, out of his belly shall flow rivers of living water.

JOHN 7:38

DESTROYING STRONGHOLDS

You have broken down all his hedges; You have brought his strong holds to ruin.   PSALM 89:40

You have also turned the edge of his sword, and have not made him to stand in the battle. You have made his glory to cease, and cast his throne down to the ground.   PSALM 89:43–44

For though we walk in the flesh, we do not war after the flesh: (for the weapons of our warfare are not carnal, but mighty through God to the pulling down of strong holds;) casting down imaginations, and every high thing that exalts itself against the knowledge of God, and bringing into captivity every thought to the obedience of Christ.   2 CORINTHIANS 10:3–5

For we wrestle not against flesh and blood, but against principalities, against powers, against the rulers of the darkness of this world, against spiritual wickedness in high places.
                                                              EPHESIANS 6:12

For the word of God is quick, and powerful, and sharper than any two-edged sword, piercing even to the dividing asunder of soul and spirit, and of the joints and marrow, and is a discerner of the thoughts and intents of the heart.   HEBREWS 4:12

INSIGHTS ON FAITH FROM SMITH WIGGLESWORTH

Believe that God is able to work out His plan in your life. He will work mightily through you if you believe. Great possibilities are within your reach if you dare to believe.

⌒

I tell you, beloved, we can never bind the strong man until we are in the place of binding. I thank God that Satan had to come out. Yes, and how did he come out? By the Word of God's power. And, beloved, if we get to know and understand the principles of our inheritance by faith, we will find out Satan will always be cast out by the same power that cast him out in the beginning.

⌒

The man who walks with God can only afford to follow God's leadings, and when He leads you, it is direct and clear.

ENCOURAGEMENT

And the LORD *said to him, Who has made man's mouth? or Who makes the dumb, or deaf, or the seeing, or the blind? have not I the* LORD*? Now therefore go, and I will be with your mouth, and teach you what you shall say.*　　　EXODUS 4:11–12

Have not I commanded you? Be strong and of a good courage; be not afraid, neither be you dismayed: for the LORD *your God is with you wherever you go.*　　　JOSHUA 1:9

For in the time of trouble He shall hide me in His pavilion: in the secret of His tabernacle shall He hide me; He shall set me up upon a rock.　　　PSALM 27:5

The LORD *is my strength and my shield; my heart trusted in Him, and I am helped: therefore my heart greatly rejoices; and with my song will I praise Him.*　　　PSALM 28:7

Delight yourself also in the LORD*: and He shall give you the desires of your heart.*　　　PSALM 37:4

This I recall to my mind, therefore have I hope. It is of the LORD'*s mercies that we are not consumed, because His compassions fail not. They are new every morning: great is Your faithfulness.*

LAMENTATIONS 3:21–23

The Lord is good to them that wait for Him, to the soul that seeks Him.
LAMENTATIONS 3:25

For I am the Lord, I change not; therefore you sons of Jacob are not consumed.
MALACHI 3:6

Jesus said to him, If you can believe, all things are possible to him that believes.
MARK 9:23

And Jesus answering says to them, Have faith in God. For verily I say to you, That whosoever shall say to this mountain, Be you removed, and be you cast into the sea; and shall not doubt in his heart, but shall believe that those things which he says shall come to pass; he shall have whatsoever he says.
MARK 11:22–23

He staggered not at the promise of God through unbelief; but was strong in faith, giving glory to God; and being fully persuaded that, what He had promised, He was able also to perform.
ROMANS 4:20–21

That if you shall confess with your mouth the Lord Jesus, and shall believe in your heart that God has raised Him from the dead, you shall be saved.
ROMANS 10:9

Dearly beloved, avenge not yourselves, but rather give place to wrath: for it is written, Vengeance is Mine; I will repay, says the Lord.
ROMANS 12:19

Now the God of hope fill you with all joy and peace in believing, that you may abound in hope, through the power of the Holy Ghost.   ROMANS 15:13

God is faithful, by whom you were called to the fellowship of his Son Jesus Christ our Lord.   1 CORINTHIANS 1:9

Knowing that a man is not justified by the works of the law, but by the faith of Jesus Christ, even we have believed in Jesus Christ, that we might be justified by the faith of Christ, and not by the works of the law: for by the works of the law shall no flesh be justified.   GALATIANS 2:16

Now our Lord Jesus Christ himself, and God, even our Father, which has loved us, and has given us everlasting consolation and good hope through grace, Comfort your hearts, and establish you in every good word and work.   2 THESSALONIANS 2:16–17

But rejoice, inasmuch as you are partakers of Christ's sufferings; that, when His glory shall be revealed, you may be glad also with exceeding joy. If you be reproached for the name of Christ, happy are you; for the Spirit of glory and of God rests upon you: on their part He is evil spoken of, but on your part He is glorified.
                                    1 PETER 4:13–14

INSIGHTS ON FAITH FROM SMITH WIGGLESWORTH

Romans says it is by faith, that it might be by grace. Grace is omnipotence; it is activity, benevolence, and mercy. It is truth, perfection, and God's inheritance in the soul that can believe. God gives us a negative side. What is it? It is by faith. Grace is God. You open the door by faith, and God comes in with all you need and want. It cannot be otherwise, for it is *"of faith that it might be according to grace"* (Rom. 4:16). It cannot be by grace unless you say it will be so.

◡⌐

Take the Word of God; it will furnish you in every good stand; it is there. You will find out you want nothing better; there is nothing better. It is there—you will find all you want: food for hunger, light for darkness, largeness of heart, conceptions of thought, inspiration.

◡⌐

These are days when we need to have our faith strengthened, when we need to know God. God has designed that the just will live by faith (Rom. 1:17), no matter how he may be fettered. I know that God's Word is sufficient. One word from Him can change a nation. His Word is *"from everlasting to everlasting"* (Ps. 90:2).

GOD'S FAVOR

And I will establish My covenant between Me and you and your seed after you in their generations for an everlasting covenant, to be a God to you, and to your seed after you. GENESIS 17:7

By this I know that You favor me, because my enemy does not triumph over me. PSALM 41:11

Blessed be the Lord, who daily loads us with benefits, even the God of our salvation. PSALM 68:19

Bless the LORD, you His angels, that excel in strength, that do His commandments, hearkening to the voice of His word.
PSALM 103:20

Remember me, O LORD, with the favor that You bear to Your people: O visit me with Your salvation. PSALM 106:4

In the fear of the LORD is strong confidence: and his children shall have a place of refuge. The fear of the LORD is a fountain of life, to depart from the snares of death. PROVERBS 14:26–27

When you pass through the waters, I will be with you; and through the rivers, they shall not overflow you: when you walk through the fire, you shall not be burned; neither shall the flame kindle upon you. ISAIAH 43:2

To proclaim the acceptable year of the LORD, and the day of vengeance of our God; to comfort all that mourn. ISAIAH 61:2

And Mary said, My soul does magnify the Lord. And my spirit has rejoiced in God my Savior. For He has regarded the low estate of His handmaiden: for, behold, from hereafter all generations shall call me blessed. For He that is mighty has done to me great things; and holy is His name. And His mercy is on them that fear Him from generation to generation. LUKE 1: 46–50

For the weapons of our warfare are not carnal, but mighty through God to the pulling down of strong holds.
2 CORINTHIANS 10:4

Stand therefore, having your loins girt about with truth, and having on the breastplate of righteousness; and your feet shod with the preparation of the gospel of peace; above all, taking the shield of faith, wherewith you shall be able to quench all the fiery darts of the wicked. And take the helmet of salvation, and the sword of the Spirit, which is the word of God. EPHESIANS 6:14–17

Therefore being justified by faith, we have peace with God through our Lord Jesus Christ. ROMANS 5:1

FINDING GOD IN HARD TIMES

Say to them that are of a fearful heart, Be strong, fear not: behold, your God will come with vengeance, even God with a recompence; He will come and save you.   ISAIAH 35:4

As for God, His way is perfect: the word of the LORD is tried: He is a buckler to all those that trust in Him.   PSALM 18:30

Yea, though I walk through the valley of the shadow of death, I will fear no evil: for You are with me; Your rod and Your staff they comfort me.   PSALM 23:4

The LORD shall preserve you from all evil: He shall preserve your soul. The LORD shall preserve your going out and your coming in from this time forth, and even for evermore.   PSALM 121:7–8

And call upon Me in the day of trouble: I will deliver you, and you shall glorify Me.   PSALM 50:15

Every valley shall be filled, and every mountain and hill shall be brought low; and the crooked shall be made straight, and the rough ways shall be made smooth.   LUKE 3:5

INSIGHTS ON FAITH FROM SMITH WIGGLESWORTH

None of you can be strong in God unless you are diligently and constantly listening to what God has to say to you through His Word. You cannot know the power and the nature of God unless you partake of His inbreathed Word. Read it in the morning, in the evening, and at every opportunity you get.

◡

We do not have to go down to bring Him up or up to bring Him down. He is near to you. He is in your heart. It is a living word of faith that we preach. (See Romans 10:6–8.) God wants you all to know that if you only dare to act upon the divine principle that is written there, the gates of hell will not prevail. Praise the Lord.

◡

God wants daring men: men who will dare all, men who will be strong in Him and dare to do exploits. How will we reach this place of faith? Give up your own mind. Let go of your own thoughts, and take the thoughts of God, the Word of God. If you build yourself on imaginations, you will go wrong. You have the Word of God, and it is enough.

GOD'S PRESENCE

And He said, My presence shall go with you, and I will give you rest. Exodus 33:14

For the Lord *your God is a merciful God; He will not forsake You, neither destroy you, nor forget the covenant of your fathers which He swore to them.* Deuteronomy 4:31

For the Lord *will not forsake His people for His great name's sake: because it has pleased the* Lord *to make you His people.* 1 Samuel 12:22

And they that know Your name will put their trust in You: for You, Lord, *have not forsaken them that seek you.* Psalm 9:10

Oh how great is Your goodness, which You have laid up for them that fear You; which You have wrought for them that trust in You before the sons of men! You shall hide them in the secret of Your presence from the pride of man: You shall keep them secretly in a pavilion from the strife of tongues. Psalm 31:19–20

The eyes of the Lord *are upon the righteous, and His ears are open to their cry.... The righteous cry, and the* Lord *hears, and delivers them out of all their troubles.* Psalm 34:15, 17

He shall call upon Me, and I will answer him: I will be with him in trouble; I will deliver him, and honor him. With long life will I satisfy him, and show him My salvation. PSALM 91:15–16

Where shall I go from Your Spirit? or where shall I flee from Your presence? If I ascend up into heaven, You are there: if I make my bed in hell, behold, You are there. If I take the wings of the morning, and dwell in the uttermost parts of the sea; even there shall Your hand lead me, and Your right hand shall hold me.
PSALM 139:7–10

Fear you not; for I am with you: be not dismayed; for I am Your God: I will strengthen you; yea, I will help you; yea, I will uphold you with the right hand of My righteousness. ISAIAH 41:10

Behold, I have graven you upon the palms of My hands; your walls are continually before Me. ISAIAH 49:16

For the mountains shall depart, and the hills be removed; but My kindness shall not depart from you, neither shall the covenant of My peace be removed, says the LORD that has mercy on you.
ISAIAH 54:10

And you shall seek Me, and find Me, when you shall search for Me with all your heart. JEREMIAH 29:13

Teaching them to observe all things whatsoever I have commanded you: and, lo, I am with you always, even to the end of the world. Amen.   MATTHEW 28:20

Abide in Me, and I in you. As the branch cannot bear fruit of itself, except it abide in the vine; no more can you, except you abide in Me.   JOHN 15:4

As the Father has loved Me, so have I loved you: continue you in My love.   JOHN 15:9

Draw near to God, and He will draw near to you. Cleanse your hands, you sinners; and purify your hearts, you double minded.

JAMES 4:8

No man has seen God at any time. If we love one another, God dwells in us, and His love is perfected in us.

1 JOHN 4:12

And I heard a great voice out of heaven saying, Behold, the tabernacle of God is with men, and He will dwell with them, and they shall be His people, and God Himself shall be with them, and be their God.   REVELATION 21:3

INSIGHTS ON FAITH FROM SMITH WIGGLESWORTH

Never be afraid of anything. There are two things in the world: one is fear, the other faith. One belongs to the devil; the other to God. If you believe in God, there is no fear. If you sway toward any delusion of Satan, you will be brought into fear. Fear always brings bondage.

⌒

There is something different between saying you have faith and then being pressed into a tight corner and proving that you have faith. If you dare to believe, it will be done according to your faith: *"Whatever things you ask when you pray, believe that you receive them, and you will have them"* (Mark 11:24).

⌒

You know, beloved, there are many wonderful treasures in the storehouse of God that we have not yet gotten to. But praise God, we have the promise in Corinthians: *"Eye has not seen, nor ear heard, nor have entered into the heart of man the things which God has prepared for those who love Him"* (1 Cor. 2:9).

JOY & GLADNESS

You will show me the path of life: in Your presence is fullness of joy; at Your right hand there are pleasures for evermore.

PSALM 16:11

Be glad in the LORD, and rejoice, you righteous: and shout for joy, all you that are upright in heart. PSALM 32:11

My soul shall be satisfied as with marrow and fatness; and my mouth shall praise You with joyful lips. PSALM 63:5

The righteous shall be glad in the LORD, and shall trust in Him; and all the upright in heart shall glory. PSALM 64:10

Let all those that seek You rejoice and be glad in You: and let such as love Your salvation say continually, Let God be magnified.

PSALM 70:4

Blessed is the people that know the joyful sound: they shall walk, O LORD, in the light of Your countenance. In Your name shall they rejoice all the day: and in Your righteousness shall they be exalted. PSALM 89:15–16

Make a joyful noise to the LORD, all you lands. Serve the LORD with gladness: come before His presence with singing.

PSALM 100:1–2

They that sow in tears shall reap in joy. He that goes forth and weeps, bearing precious seed, shall doubtless come again with rejoicing, bringing his sheaves with him. PSALM 126:5–6

For you shall go out with joy, and be led forth with peace: the mountains and the hills shall break forth before you into singing, and all the trees of the field shall clap their hands.

ISAIAH 55:12

I will greatly rejoice in the LORD, my soul shall be joyful in my God; for He has clothed me with the garments of salvation, He has covered me with the robe of righteousness, as a bridegroom decks himself with ornaments, and as a bride adorns herself with her jewels. ISAIAH 61:10

Until now have you asked nothing in My name: ask, and you shall receive, that your joy may be full. JOHN 16:24

Rejoice in the Lord always: and again I say, Rejoice.

PHILIPPIANS 4:4

PATIENCE

Though I walk in the midst of trouble, You will revive me: You shall stretch forth Your hand against the wrath of my enemies, and Your right hand shall save me. PSALM 138:7

That you be not slothful, but followers of them who through faith and patience inherit the promises. HEBREWS 6:12

And not only so, but we glory in tribulations also: knowing that tribulation works patience; and patience, experience; and experience, hope: and hope makes not ashamed; because the love of God is shed abroad in our hearts by the Holy Ghost which is given to us. ROMANS 5:3–5

My brethren, count it all joy when you fall into divers temptations; knowing this, that the trying of your faith works patience. But let patience have her perfect work, that you may be perfect and entire, wanting nothing. If any of you lack wisdom, let him ask of God, that gives to all men liberally, and upbraids not; and it shall be given him. But let him ask in faith, nothing wavering. For he that wavers is like a wave of the sea driven with the wind and tossed. For let not that man think that he shall receive any thing of the Lord. A double minded man is unstable in all his ways. JAMES 1:2–8

INSIGHTS ON FAITH FROM SMITH WIGGLESWORTH

God wants us to have far more than what we can handle and see, and so He speaks of *"the substance of things hoped for, the evidence of things not seen"* (Heb. 11:1). With the eye of faith, we may see the blessing in all its beauty and grandeur. God's Word is from everlasting to everlasting, and "faith is the substance."

Oh, there is faith, the faith that is in me. And Jesus wants to bring us all into a place in line with God where we cease to be, for God must have the right of way, of thought, and of purpose. God must have the way.

The great need today is more of the Word. There is no foundation apart from the Word. The Word not only gives you foundation, but it puts you in a place where you can stand and, after the battle, keep on standing. Nothing else will do it. When the Word is in your heart, it will preserve you from desire of sin. The Word is the living presence of that divine power that overcomes the world. You need the Word of God in your hearts that you might be able to overcome the world.

PROVISION GIFTS

Therefore I say to you, What things soever you desire, when you pray, believe that you receive them, and you shall have them.

Mark 11:24

If you then, being evil, know how to give good gifts to your children: how much more shall your heavenly Father give the Holy Spirit to them that ask Him?

Luke 11:13

And God is able to make all grace abound toward you; that you, always having all sufficiency in all things, may abound to every good work.

2 Corinthians 9:8

For by grace are you saved through faith; and that not of yourselves: it is the gift of God.

Ephesians 2:8

Every good gift and every perfect gift is from above, and comes down from the Father of lights, with whom is no variableness, neither shadow of turning.

James 1:17

As every man has received the gift, even so minister the same one to another, as good stewards of the manifold grace of God.

1 Peter 4:10

TIMES OF UNCERTAINTY

Trust in the LORD *with all your heart; and lean not to your own understanding. In all your ways acknowledge Him, and He shall direct your paths. Be not wise in your own eyes: fear the* LORD, *and depart from evil. It shall be health to your navel, and marrow to your bones.*　　　　　　　　　　　PROVERBS 3:5–8

Yet I will rejoice in the LORD, *I will joy in the God of my salvation.*　　　　　　　　　　　　　　　　HABAKKUK 3:18

Wherefore, if God so clothe the grass of the field, which to day is, and to morrow is cast into the oven, shall He not much more clothe you, O you of little faith? Therefore take no thought, saying, What shall we eat? or, What shall we drink? or, Wherewithal shall we be clothed? (For after all these things do the Gentiles seek:) for your heavenly Father knows that you have need of all these things.　　　　　　　　　　MATTHEW 6:30–32

For we are saved by hope: but hope that is seen is not hope: for what a man sees, why does he yet hope for? But if we hope for that we see not, then do we with patience wait for it.
　　　　　　　　　　　　　　　　ROMANS 8:24–25

Who shall separate us from the love of Christ? shall tribulation, or distress, or persecution, or famine, or nakedness, or peril, or sword?... Nay, in all these things we are more than conquerors through Him that loved us. For I am persuaded, that neither death, nor life, nor angels, nor principalities, nor powers, nor things present, nor things to come, nor height, nor depth, nor any other creature, shall be able to separate us from the love of God, which is in Christ Jesus our Lord. ROMANS 8:35, 37–39

For whosoever shall call upon the name of the Lord shall be saved. ROMANS 10:13

But my God shall supply all your need according to His riches in glory by Christ Jesus. PHILIPPIANS 4:19

My brethren, count it all joy when you fall into divers temptations; knowing this, that the trying of your faith works patience. JAMES 1:2–3

Behold, I stand at the door, and knock: if any man hear My voice, and open the door, I will come in to him, and will sup with him, and he with Me. REVELATION 3:20

INSIGHTS ON FAITH FROM SMITH WIGGLESWORTH

God brings us into a place of perfect love and perfect faith. A man who is born of God is brought into an inward affection, a loyalty to the Lord Jesus that shrinks from anything impure. You see the purity of a man and woman when there is a deep natural affection between them; they disdain the very thought of either of them being untrue. In the same way, in the measure that a man has faith in Jesus, he is pure. He who believes that Jesus is the Christ overcomes the world. It is a faith that works by love.

<hr/>

I believe the Word of God is so powerful that it can transform any and every life. There is power in God's Word to make that which does not exist to appear. There is executive power in the words that proceed from His lips.

<hr/>

There is no limit to the power God will cause to come upon those who cry to Him in faith, for God is rich to all who will call upon Him. Stake your claim for your children, your families, your coworkers, that many sons may be brought to glory. As your prayer rests upon the simple principle of faith, nothing will be impossible for you.

"FOR GOD'S WORD IS:
SUPERNATURAL IN ORIGIN. ETERNAL IN
DURATION. INEXPRESSIBLE IN VALOR.
INFINITE IN SCOPE. REGENERATIVE IN POWER.
INFALLIBLE IN AUTHORITY. UNIVERSAL IN
APPLICATION. INSPIRED IN TOTALITY.
WE SHOULD:
READ IT THROUGH. WRITE IT DOWN.
PRAY IT IN. WORK IT OUT. PASS IT ON."
—SMITH WIGGLESWORTH

4

POWER OF FAITH IN SCRIPTURE

FAITH IN GOD'S POWER

Your right hand, O LORD, is become glorious in power: Your right hand, O LORD, has dashed in pieces the enemy.

EXODUS 15:6

Be still, and know that I am God: I will be exalted among the heathen, I will be exalted in the earth.   **PSALM 46:10**

He rules by His power for ever; His eyes behold the nations: let not the rebellious exalt themselves.   **PSALM 66:7**

He shall call upon Me, and I will answer him: I will be with him in trouble; I will deliver him, and honor him. With long life will I satisfy him, and show him My salvation.   **PSALM 91:15–16**

For the mountains shall depart, and the hills be removed; but My kindness shall not depart from you, neither shall the covenant of My peace be removed, says the Lord that has mercy on you.

ISAIAH 54:10

Abide in Me, and I in you. As the branch cannot bear fruit of itself, except it abide in the vine; no more can you, except you abide in Me.

JOHN 15:4

Through mighty signs and wonders, by the power of the Spirit of God; so that from Jerusalem, and round about to Illyricum, I have fully preached the gospel of Christ.

ROMANS 15:19

And my speech and my preaching was not with enticing words of man's wisdom, but in demonstration of the Spirit and of power.

1 CORINTHIANS 2:4

For God, who commanded the light to shine out of darkness, has shined in our hearts, to give the light of the knowledge of the glory of God in the face of Jesus Christ.

2 CORINTHIANS 4:6

Whereas angels, which are greater in power and might, bring not railing accusation against them before the Lord.

2 PETER 2:11

INSIGHTS ON FAITH FROM SMITH WIGGLESWORTH

Jesus became the Author of faith. God worked the plan through Him by forming the worlds and making everything that there was by the Word of His power. Jesus Christ was the Word. God so manifested this power in the world, forming the worlds by the word of Jesus.

The Word of God is for us. It is by faith, so that it might be by grace.

The Word of God will bring you into a wonderful place of rest in faith. God intends for you to have a clear conception of what faith is, how faith came, and how it remains. Faith is in the divine plan, for it brings you to the open door so that you might enter in.

FAITH IN GOD'S WORDS

Therefore shall you lay up these My words in your heart and in your soul, and bind them for a sign upon your hand, that they may be as frontlets between your eyes.　　Deuteronomy 11:18

This book of the law shall not depart out of your mouth; but you shall meditate therein day and night, that you may observe to do according to all that is written therein: for then you shall make your way prosperous, and then you shall have good success.

Joshua 1:8

Thy word is a lamp to my feet, and a light to my path.

Psalm 119:105

The entrance of Your words gives light; it gives understanding to the simple.　　Psalm 119:130

For the commandment is a lamp; and the law is light; and reproofs of instruction are the way of life.　　Proverbs 6:23

And you shall seek Me, and find Me, when you shall search for Me with all your heart.　　Jeremiah 29:13

Are You greater than our father Jacob, which gave us the well, and drank thereof himself, and his children, and his cattle?

John 4:12

Search the scriptures; for in them you think you have eternal life: and they are they which testify of Me.　　　　JOHN 5:39

And now, brethren, I commend you to God, and to the word of His grace, which is able to build you up, and to give you an inheritance among all them which are sanctified.　　　　ACTS 20:32

For I am not ashamed of the gospel of Christ: for it is the power of God to salvation to every one that believes; to the Jew first, and also to the Greek.　　　　ROMANS 1:16

So then faith comes by hearing, and hearing by the word of God.　　　　ROMANS 10:17

And that from a child you have known the holy scriptures, which are able to make you wise to salvation through faith which is in Christ Jesus. All scripture is given by inspiration of God, and is profitable for doctrine, for reproof, for correction, for instruction in righteousness.　　　　2 TIMOTHY 3:15–16

For the word of God is quick, and powerful, and sharper than any two-edged sword, piercing even to the dividing asunder of soul and spirit, and of the joints and marrow, and is a discerner of the thoughts and intents of the heart.　　　　HEBREWS 4:12

But be you doers of the word, and not hearers only, deceiving your own selves. For if any be a hearer of the word, and not a doer, he is like to a man beholding his natural face in a glass. For he beholds himself, and goes his way, and immediately forgets what manner of man he was.   JAMES 1:22–24

As newborn babes, desire the sincere milk of the word, that you may grow thereby.   1 PETER 2:2

Being born again, not of corruptible seed, but of incorruptible, by the word of God, which lives and abides for ever.

1 PETER 1:23

We have also a more sure word of prophecy; whereto you do well that you take heed, as to a light that shines in a dark place, until the day dawn, and the day star arise in your hearts.

2 PETER 1:19

Blessed is he that reads, and they that hear the words of this prophecy, and keep those things which are written therein: for the time is at hand.   REVELATION 1:3

INSIGHTS ON FAITH FROM SMITH WIGGLESWORTH

God's Word is a tremendous word, a productive word. It produces what it is—power. It produces Godlikeness. We get to heaven through Christ, the Word of God; we have peace through the blood of His cross. Redemption is ours through the knowledge of the Word.

⌒

Nothing in the world glorifies God as much as simple rest of faith in what God's Word says. *"This is the work of God, that you believe"* (John 6:29).

⌒

The Bible is truth; it is the Word of God; it is God Himself portrayed in Word. You see God in the Word. God can manifest Himself through that Word until we become a living factor of that truth because *"God is light and in Him is no darkness"* (1 John 1:5). God is life. God is revelation. God is manifestation. God is operation. So God wants to truly bring us into a place where we have the clearest revelation—even though there may be much conviction through it—the clearest revelation of where we stand.

FAITH IN JESUS' NAME

And Jesus came and spoke to them, saying, All power is given to Me in heaven and in earth.　　　　　MATTHEW 28:18

Jesus said to her, I am the resurrection, and the life: he that believes in Me, though he were dead, yet shall he live: and whosoever lives and believes in Me shall never die. Believe you this?
　　　　　　　　　　　　　　　　　JOHN 11:25–26

Behold, I give to you power to tread on serpents and scorpions, and over all the power of the enemy: and nothing shall by any means hurt you.　　　　　LUKE 10:19

And in that day you shall ask Me nothing. Verily, verily, I say to you, Whatsoever you shall ask the Father in My name, He will give it you.　　　　　JOHN 16:23

Then Peter said to them, Repent, and be baptized every one of you in the name of Jesus Christ for the remission of sins, and you shall receive the gift of the Holy Ghost.　　　　　ACTS 2:38

Then Peter said, Silver and gold have I none; but such as I have give I you: in the name of Jesus Christ of Nazareth rise up and walk.　　　　　ACTS 3:6

That if you shall confess with your mouth the Lord Jesus, and shall believe in your heart that God has raised Him from the dead, you shall be saved.   ROMANS 10:9

For none of us lives to himself, and no man dies to himself. For whether we live, we live to the Lord; and whether we die, we die to the Lord: whether we live therefore, or die, we are the Lord's.
                                        ROMANS 14:7–8

Wherefore God also has highly exalted Him, and given Him a name which is above every name: that at the name of Jesus every knee should bow, of things in heaven, and things in earth, and things under the earth; and that every tongue should confess that Jesus Christ is Lord, to the glory of God the Father.
                                        PHILIPPIANS 2:9–11

He that commits sin is of the devil; for the devil sins from the beginning. For this purpose the Son of God was manifested, that He might destroy the works of the devil.   1 JOHN 3:8

And we have seen and do testify that the Father sent the Son to be the Savior of the world.   1 JOHN 4:14

ACCOUNTS OF FAITH IN SCRIPTURE

David said moreover, The Lord that delivered me out of the paw of the lion, and out of the paw of the bear, He will deliver me out of the hand of this Philistine. And Saul said to David, Go, and the Lord be with you.   1 Samuel 17:37

Have you not known? have you not heard, that the everlasting God, the Lord, the Creator of the ends of the earth, faints not, neither is weary? there is no searching of His understanding. He gives power to the faint; and to them that have no might he increases strength.   Isaiah 40:28–29

For My thoughts are not your thoughts, neither are your ways My ways, says the Lord. For as the heavens are higher than the earth, so are My ways higher than your ways, and My thoughts than your thoughts.   Isaiah 55:8–9

Lord, how are they increased that trouble me! many are they that rise up against me. Many there be which say of my soul, There is no help for him in God. Selah. But You, O Lord, are a shield for me; my glory, and the lifter up of my head.   Psalm 3:1–3

I cried to the Lord with my voice, and He heard me out of His holy hill. Selah. I laid me down and slept; I awakened; for the Lord sustained me.   Psalm 3:4–5

Be still, and know that I am God: I will be exalted among the heathen, I will be exalted in the earth.　　　PSALM 46:10

And when Jesus was entered into Capernaum, there came to Him a centurion, beseeching Him, and saying, Lord, my servant lies at home sick of the palsy, grievously tormented. And Jesus says to him, I will come and heal him. The centurion answered and said, Lord, I am not worthy that You should come under my roof: but speak the word only, and my servant shall be healed. For I am a man under authority, having soldiers under me: and I say to this man, Go, and he goes; and to another, Come, and he comes; and to my servant, Do this, and he does it. When Jesus heard it, he marveled, and said to them that followed, Verily I say to you, I have not found so great faith, no, not in Israel.　　　MATTHEW 8:5–10

And, behold, a woman, which was diseased with an issue of blood twelve years, came behind Him, and touched the hem of His garment: for she said within herself, If I may but touch His garment, I shall be whole. But Jesus turned Him about, and when He saw her, He said, Daughter, be of good comfort; your faith has made you whole. And the woman was made whole from that hour.　　　MATTHEW 9:20–22

INSIGHTS ON FAITH FROM SMITH WIGGLESWORTH

God has a way to bring us to faith, and it never comes by any human means. It always comes by divine principles. You cannot know God by nature; you get to know God by an open door of grace. He has made a way. It is a beautiful way so that all His saints can enter in by that way and find rest. The way is the way of faith; there isn't any other way. If you climb up any other way, you cannot work it out.

⌒

And truly the Word of God changes a man until he becomes an epistle of God. It transforms his mind, changes his character, moves him on from grace to grace, makes him an inheritor of the very nature of God. God comes in, dwells in, walks in, talks through, and dines with him who opens his being to the Word of God and receives the Spirit who inspired it.

⌒

Everyone is changed by this faith from grace to grace. We become divine inheritors of the promises, and we become the substance. There is one ideal only, and that is that God is working in this holy principle of faith. It is divine.

ACCOUNTS OF FAITH IN SCRIPTURE

Then touched He their eyes, saying, According to your faith be it to you.   MATTHEW 9:29

Which indeed is the least of all seeds: but when it is grown, it is the greatest among herbs, and becomes a tree, so that the birds of the air come and lodge in the branches thereof.
MATTHEW 13:32

Then came she and worshipped Him, saying, Lord, help me. But He answered and said, It is not meet to take the children's bread, and to cast it to dogs. And she said, Truth, Lord: yet the dogs eat of the crumbs which fall from their masters' table. Then Jesus answered and said to her, O woman, great is your faith: be it to you even as you will. And her daughter was made whole from that very hour.   MATTHEW 15:25–28

Then said Jesus to him, Put up again your sword into his place: for all they that take the sword shall perish with the sword. Think you that I cannot now pray to My Father, and He shall presently give Me more than twelve legions of angels? But how then shall the scriptures be fulfilled, that thus it must be?
MATTHEW 26:52–54

And He was in the hinder part of the ship, asleep on a pillow: and they awake Him, and say to Him, Master, care You not that we perish? And He arose, and rebuked the wind, and said to the sea, Peace, be still. And the wind ceased, and there was a great calm. And He said to them, Why are you so fearful? How is it that you have no faith? And they feared exceedingly, and said one to another, What manner of man is this, that even the wind and the sea obey Him? MARK 4:38–41

As soon as Jesus heard the word that was spoken, He said to the ruler of the synagogue, Be not afraid, only believe. MARK 5:36

He that believes and is baptized shall be saved; but he that believes not shall be damned. MARK 16:16

For they were about five thousand men. And He said to his disciples, Make them sit down by fifties in a company. And they did so, and made them all sit down. Then He took the five loaves and the two fishes, and looking up to heaven, He blessed them, and broke, and gave to the disciples to set before the multitude. LUKE 9:14–16

And the Lord said, Simon, Simon, behold, Satan has desired to have you, that he may sift you as wheat: but I have prayed for you, that your faith fail not: and when you are converted, strengthen your brethren. LUKE 22:31–32

Verily, verily, I say to you, The hour is coming, and now is, when the dead shall hear the voice of the Son of God: and they that hear shall live.   JOHN 5:25

For My flesh is meat indeed, and My blood is drink indeed. He that eats my flesh, and drinks My blood, dwells in Me, and I in him. As the living Father has sent Me, and I live by the Father: so he that eats Me, even he shall live by Me. This is that bread which came down from heaven: not as your fathers did eat manna, and are dead: he that eats of this bread shall live for ever. These things said He in the synagogue, as he taught in Capernaum.   JOHN 6:55–59

Jesus says to him, Thomas, because you have seen Me, you have believed: blessed are they that have not seen, and yet have believed.   JOHN 20:29

But these are written, that you might believe that Jesus is the Christ, the Son of God; and that believing you might have life through His name.   JOHN 20:31

INSIGHTS ON FAITH FROM SMITH WIGGLESWORTH

God has saved us with this Word of power over the powers of sin. I know there is a teaching and a need of teaching of the personality of the presence of the fidelity of the Word of God with power. And we need to eat and drink of this Word. We need to feed upon it in our hearts.

⌒

All our movements, and all that ever will come to us that is of any importance, will be because we have a Rock. And if you are on the Rock, no powers can move you. And today we need to have our faith firmly built upon the Rock. In any area or principle of your faith, you must have something established in you to bring it forth. And there is no establishment outside God's Word for you. Everything else is sand. Everything else will break apart.

⌒

I believe that there is only one way to all the treasures of God, and it is the way of faith. There is only one principle underlying all the attributes and all the beatitudes of the mighty ascension into the glories of Christ, and it is faith. All the promises are "Yes" and "Amen" to those who believe.

ACCOUNTS OF FAITH IN SCRIPTURE

Therefore we are buried with Him by baptism into death: that like as Christ was raised up from the dead by the glory of the Father, even so we also should walk in newness of life. ROMANS 6:4

Watch you, stand fast in the faith, quit you like men, be strong. 1 CORINTHIANS 16:13

Is the law then against the promises of God? God forbid: for if there had been a law given which could have given life, verily righteousness should have been by the law. GALATIANS 3:21

By faith Noah, being warned of God of things not seen as yet, moved with fear, prepared an ark to the saving of his house; by the which he condemned the world, and became heir of the righteousness which is by faith. HEBREWS 11:7

Simon Peter, a servant and an apostle of Jesus Christ, to them that have obtained like precious faith with us through the righteousness of God and our Saviour Jesus Christ. 2 PETER 1:1

But sanctify the Lord God in your hearts: and be ready always to give an answer to every man that asks you a reason of the hope that is in you with meekness and fear. 1 PETER 3:15

POWER OF SCRIPTURE

This book of the law shall not depart out of your mouth; but you shall meditate therein day and night, that you may observe to do according to all that is written therein: for then you shall make your way prosperous, and then you shall have good success.

JOSHUA 1:8

And the Spirit of God came upon Zechariah the son of Jehoiada the priest, which stood above the people, and said to them, Thus says God, Why transgress you the commandments of the LORD, that you cannot prosper? because you have forsaken the LORD, He has also forsaken you.

2 CHRONICLES 24:20

So shall My word be that goes forth out of My mouth: it shall not return to Me void, but it shall accomplish that which I please, and it shall prosper in the thing whereto I sent it.

ISAIAH 55:11

Your words were found, and I did eat them; and Your word was to me the joy and rejoicing of my heart: for I am called by Your name, O LORD God of hosts.

JEREMIAH 15:16

Is not My word like as a fire? says the LORD; and like a hammer that breaks the rock in pieces?

JEREMIAH 23:29

The law of the LORD is perfect, converting the soul: the testimony of the LORD is sure, making wise the simple.

PSALM 19:7

The fear of the LORD is clean, enduring for ever: the judgments of the LORD are true and righteous altogether. More to be desired are they than gold, yea, than much fine gold: sweeter also than honey and the honeycomb. Moreover by them is Your servant warned: and in keeping of them there is great reward.

PSALM 19:9–11

By the word of the LORD were the heavens made; and all the host of them by the breath of his mouth.   PSALM 33:6

He sent His word, and healed them, and delivered them from their destructions.   PSALM 107:20

You are my hiding place and my shield: I hope in Your word.

PSALM 119:114

My son, attend to my words; incline your ear to my sayings. Let them not depart from your eyes; keep them in the midst of your heart. For they are life to those that find them, and health to all their flesh. Keep your heart with all diligence; for out of it are the issues of life.   PROVERBS 4:20–23

INSIGHTS ON FAITH FROM SMITH WIGGLESWORTH

May God give us faith that will bring this glorious inheritance into our hearts, for it is true that the just will live by faith (Rom. 1:17), and do not forget that it takes a just man to live by faith. May the Lord reveal to us the fullness of this truth that God gave to Abraham.

God spoke the Word and made the world, and I want to impress upon you this wonderful Word that made the world. I am saved by the incorruptible Word, the Word that made the world, and so my position by faith is to lay hold of the things that cannot be seen and believe the things that cannot be understood.

In weakness, strength, poverty, and wealth is this Word! It is a flame of fire. It may burn in your bones. It may move in every tissue of your body. It may bring out of you so forcibly the plan and purpose and life of God until you cease to be, for God has taken you.

POWER OF SCRIPTURE

And the king went up into the house of the LORD, and all the men of Judah and all the inhabitants of Jerusalem with him, and the priests, and the prophets, and all the people, both small and great: and he read in their ears all the words of the book of the covenant which was found in the house of the LORD. And the king stood by a pillar, and made a covenant before the LORD, to walk after the LORD, and to keep His commandments and His testimonies and His statutes with all their heart and all their soul, to perform the words of this covenant that were written in this book. And all the people stood to the covenant. 2 KINGS 23:2–3

But He answered and said, It is written, Man shall not live by bread alone, but by every word that proceeds out of the mouth of God. MATTHEW 4:4

Then says Jesus to him, Get you from here, Satan: for it is written, You shall worship the Lord your God, and Him only shall you serve. MATTHEW 4:10

For verily I say to you, Till heaven and earth pass, one jot or one tittle shall in no wise pass from the law, till all be fulfilled. MATTHEW 5:18

And said to them, It is written, My house shall be called the house of prayer; but you have made it a den of thieves. MATTHEW 21:13

Jesus answered and said to them, You do err, not knowing the scriptures, nor the power of God. Matthew 22:29

That upon you may come all the righteous blood shed upon the earth, from the blood of righteous Abel to the blood of Zacharias son of Barachias, whom you slew between the temple and the altar. Matthew 23:35

Then says Jesus to them, All you shall be offended because of Me this night: for it is written, I will smite the shepherd, and the sheep of the flock shall be scattered abroad. Matthew 26:31

Abraham says to him, They have Moses and the prophets; let them hear them. Luke 16:29

And He said to them, These are the words which I spoke to you, while I was yet with you, that all things must be fulfilled, which were written in the law of Moses, and in the prophets, and in the psalms, concerning Me. Luke 24:44

Search the scriptures; for in them you think you have eternal life: and they are they which testify of Me. John 5:39

If He called them gods, to whom the word of God came, and the scripture cannot be broken. John 10:35

Sanctify them through Your truth: Your word is truth.

JOHN 17:17

This is the disciple which testifies of these things, and wrote these things: and we know that his testimony is true. And there are also many other things which Jesus did, the which, if they should be written every one, I suppose that even the world itself could not contain the books that should be written. Amen.

JOHN 21:24–25

God has fulfilled the same to us their children, in that He has raised up Jesus again; as it is also written in the second psalm, You are my Son, this day have I begotten You. ACTS 13:33

Then said Paul, I knew not, brethren, that he was the high priest: for it is written, Thou shall not speak evil of the ruler of your people. ACTS 23:5

And when they agreed not among themselves, they departed, after that Paul had spoken one word, Well spoke the Holy Ghost by Isaiah the prophet to our fathers. ACTS 28:25

For therein is the righteousness of God revealed from faith to faith: as it is written, The just shall live by faith. ROMANS 1:17

INSIGHTS ON FAITH FROM SMITH WIGGLESWORTH

There we have the foundation of all things, which is the Word. It is a substance; it is a power. It is more than relationship; it is personality. It is a divine injunction to every soul that enters into this privilege to be born of this Word. What it means to us will be very important for us. For remember, it is a *"substance"*; it is an *"evidence of things not seen"* (Heb. 11:1). It brings about what you cannot see. It brings forth what is not there, and it takes away what is there and substitutes for it.

⁓

God took the Word and made the world.

⁓

Now, you will clearly see that God wants to bring us to a foundation. If we are ever going to make any progress in the divine life, we will have to have a real foundation. And there is no foundation except the foundation of faith for us.

POWER OF SCRIPTURE

For the invisible things of Him from the creation of the world are clearly seen, being understood by the things that are made, even His eternal power and Godhead; so that they are without excuse.   Romans 1:20

For whatsoever things were written beforetime were written for our learning, that we through patience and comfort of the scriptures might have hope.   Romans 15:4

God forbid: yea, let God be true, but every man a liar; as it is written, That You might be justified in Your sayings, and might overcome when You are judged.   Romans 3:4

As it is written, There is none righteous, no, not one.
                    Romans 3:10

(As it is written, I have made you a father of many nations,) before Him whom he believed, even God, who makes alive the dead, and calls those things which be not as though they were.
                    Romans 4:17

So then faith comes by hearing, and hearing by the word of God.
                    Romans 10:17

Through faith we understand that the worlds were framed by the word of God, so that things which are seen were not made of things which do appear. Hebrews 11:3

For the word of God is quick, and powerful, and sharper than any two-edged sword, piercing even to the dividing asunder of soul and spirit, and of the joints and marrow, and is a discerner of the thoughts and intents of the heart. Neither is there any creature that is not manifest in His sight: but all things are naked and opened to the eyes of Him with whom we have to do. Seeing then that we have a great high priest, that is passed into the heavens, Jesus the Son of God, let us hold fast our profession. Hebrews 4:12–14

But without faith it is impossible to please Him: for he that comes to God must believe that He is, and that He is a rewarder of them that diligently seek Him. Hebrews 11:6

Study to show yourself approved to God, a workman that needs not be ashamed, rightly dividing the word of truth. 2 Timothy 2:15

And that from a child you have known the holy scriptures, which are able to make you wise to salvation through faith which is in Christ Jesus. All scripture is given by inspiration of God, and is profitable for doctrine, for reproof, for correction, for instruction in righteousness: that the man of God may be perfect, thoroughly furnished to all good works. 2 TIMOTHY 3:15–17

For if any be a hearer of the word, and not a doer, he is like to a man beholding his natural face in a glass: for he beholds himself, and goes his way, and straightway forgets what manner of man he was. But whoso looks into the perfect law of liberty, and continues therein, he being not a forgetful hearer, but a doer of the work, this man shall be blessed in his deed. JAMES 1:23–25

As also in all his epistles, speaking in them of these things; in which are some things hard to be understood, which they that are unlearned and unstable wrest, as they do also the other scriptures, to their own destruction. 2 PETER 3:16

He that commits sin is of the devil; for the devil sins from the beginning. For this purpose the Son of God was manifested, that He might destroy the works of the devil. 1 JOHN 3:8

INSIGHTS ON FAITH FROM SMITH WIGGLESWORTH

Oh, that you may all allow the Word of God to have perfect victory in your bodies so that they may be tingling through and through with God's divine power! Divine life does not belong to this world but to the kingdom of heaven, and the kingdom of heaven is within you.

⌒

In the Word of God is the breath, the nature, and the power of the living God, and His power works in every person who dares to believe His Word. There is life through the power of it, and as we receive the Word of faith, we receive the nature of God Himself.

⌒

I want you to get the Word of God in your heart till the demon power has no power over you. You are over the powers of fear. Then I want you to understand that the baptism of the Holy Ghost is a love beyond any ever you had. And you are to have power after the Holy Ghost comes, and it is power over the enemy, over yourself, and over your human mind.

"GOD'S WORD NEVER SPEAKS IN VAIN.
IT ALWAYS OPENS TO YOU THE AVENUES
WHERE YOU CAN ENTER IN.
GOD OPENS THE DOOR FOR YOU.
HE SPEAKS TO YOUR HEART;
HE IS DEALING WITH YOU. "
—SMITH WIGGLESWORTH

5

A LIVING FAITH

ACCEPTING OTHERS

Behold, how good and how pleasant it is for brethren to dwell together in unity! PSALM 133:1

A man that has friends must show himself friendly: and there is a friend that sticks closer than a brother. PROVERBS 18:24

Give to him that asks you, and from him that would borrow of you turn not you away. You have heard that it has been said, You shall love your neighbor, and hate your enemy. But I say to you, Love your enemies, bless them that curse you, do good to them that hate you, and pray for them which despitefully use you, and persecute you. MATTHEW 5:42–44

For whosoever shall give you a cup of water to drink in My name, because you belong to Christ, verily I say to you, he shall not lose his reward. MARK 9:41

And as you would that men should do to you, do you also to them likewise. LUKE 6:31

For I have given you an example, that you should do as I have done to you. JOHN 13:15

This is My commandment, That you love one another, as I have loved you. Greater love has no man than this, that a man lay down his life for his friends. JOHN 15:12–13

Then Peter opened his mouth, and said, Of a truth I perceive that God is no respecter of persons: but in every nation he that fears him, and works righteousness, is accepted with Him.
ACTS 10:34–35

Be kindly affectioned one to another with brotherly love; in honor preferring one another. ROMANS 12:10

And let us consider one another to provoke to love and to good works. HEBREWS 10:24

And the Lord make you to increase and abound in love one toward another, and toward all men, even as we do toward you.
1 THESSALONIANS 3:12

If you fulfill the royal law according to the scripture, You shall love your neighbour as yourself, you do well. JAMES 2:8

AMBITION

But seek you first the kingdom of God, and His righteousness; and all these things shall be added to you. Matthew 6:33

For what is a man profited, if he shall gain the whole world, and lose his own soul? or what shall a man give in exchange for his soul? Matthew 16:26

For what is a man advantaged, if he gain the whole world, and lose himself, or be cast away? Luke 9:25

Let nothing be done through strife or vainglory; but in lowliness of mind let each esteem other better than themselves.
Philippians 2:3

And that you study to be quiet, and to do your own business, and to work with your own hands, as we commanded you; that you may walk honestly toward them that are without, and that you may have lack of nothing. 1 Thessalonians 4:11–12

For where envying and strife is, there is confusion and every evil work. James 3:16

INSIGHTS ON FAITH FROM SMITH WIGGLESWORTH

Oh, the wonderful effectiveness of God's perfect plan working in us with the divine Trinity flowing through humanity, changing our very nature to the extent that we cannot disbelieve but must act faith, talk faith, and in faith sing praises unto the Lord! There is no room for anything that is not faith, for we have passed beyond the natural plane into a new atmosphere: God enclosed and enclosing us.

◡

Faith has power to make you what God wants you to be; only you must be ready to step into the plan and believe His Word.

◡

His Word is the authority of faith. It is the living principle of faith. *"If you can believe"* (Mark 9:23), Jesus said. Believe what? Believe what the Word says. The people came and asked Jesus, *"What shall we do, that we may work the works of God?"* (John 6:28). He said, *"This is the work of God, that you believe in Him whom [God] sent"* (v. 29). *"This is the work of God."*

CALLING

Before I formed you in the belly I knew you; and before you came forth out of the womb I sanctified you, and I ordained you a prophet to the nations. Then said I, Ah, Lord GOD! behold, I cannot speak: for I am a child. But the LORD said to me, Say not, I am a child: for you shall go to all that I shall send you, and whatsoever I command you you shall speak.   JEREMIAH 1:5–6

For I know the thoughts that I think toward you, says the LORD, thoughts of peace, and not of evil, to give you an expected end.

JEREMIAH 29:11

You are the salt of the earth: but if the salt have lost his savor, wherewith shall it be salted? it is therefore good for nothing, but to be cast out, and to be trodden under foot of men.

MATTHEW 5:13

Behold, I give to you power to tread on serpents and scorpions, and over all the power of the enemy: and nothing shall by any means hurt you.   LUKE 10:19

Verily, verily, I say unto you, He that believes on Me, the works that I do shall he do also; and greater works than these shall he do; because I go to My Father.   JOHN 14:12

For as we have many members in one body, and all members have
not the same office. ROMANS 12:4

For the gifts and calling of God are without repentance.
ROMANS 11:29

When I was a child, I spoke as a child, I understood as a child, I
thought as a child: but when I became a man, I put away childish
things. 1 CORINTHIANS 13:11

For you see your calling, brethren, how that not many wise men
after the flesh, not many mighty, not many noble, are called: but
God has chosen the foolish things of the world to confound the
wise; and God has chosen the weak things of the world to confound the things which are mighty. 1 CORINTHIANS 1:26–27

But of Him are you in Christ Jesus, who of God is made to us
wisdom, and righteousness, and sanctification, and redemption.
1 CORINTHIANS 1:30

And all things are of God, who has reconciled us to Himself by
Jesus Christ, and has given to us the ministry of reconciliation;
namely, that God was in Christ, reconciling the world to Himself,
not imputing their trespasses to them; and has committed to us
the word of reconciliation. 2 CORINTHIANS 5:18–19

For by grace are you saved through faith; and that not of your-selves: it is the gift of God: not of works, lest any man should boast. For we are His workmanship, created in Christ Jesus to good works, which God has before ordained that we should walk in them.　　　　　　　　　　　　　　　　EPHESIANS 2:8–10

Till we all come in the unity of the faith, and of the knowledge of the Son of God, to a perfect man, to the measure of the stature of the fullness of Christ.　　　　　　　　　　　　　EPHESIANS 4:13

Wherefore, holy brethren, partakers of the heavenly calling, con-sider the Apostle and High Priest of our profession, Christ Jesus.　　　　　　　　　　　　　　　　　　　　　　　　HEBREWS 3:1

Wherefore the rather, brethren, give diligence to make your call-ing and election sure: for if you do these things, you shall never fall.　　　　　　　　　　　　　　　　　　　　　　2 PETER 1:10

INSIGHTS ON FAITH FROM SMITH WIGGLESWORTH

Now faith is the supreme, divine position where God is entrenched, not only in the life, but also through the life, the mind, and the body. You will never find that you are at all equal against the power of the Enemy except on the authority that you have an authority laid down within you. He who believes in his heart is able to move the mountain (Mark 11:23), but you do not believe in your heart until your heart is made perfect in the presence of God. As you think in your heart, so you are.

⌣

Have faith in God, have faith in the Son, have faith in the Holy Spirit; and the triune God will work in you to will and to do all the good pleasure of His will.

⌣

This Scripture is the Word of God, and it is most important that when we read the Word, we do so with hearts that have purposed to obey its every precept. We have no right to open the Word of God carelessly or indifferently.

CHANGE

Be strong and of a good courage, fear not, nor be afraid of them: for the LORD your God, He it is that does go with you; He will not fail you, nor forsake you.   DEUTERONOMY 31:6

To show that the LORD is upright: He is my rock, and there is no unrighteousness in Him.   PSALM 92:15

For by me your days shall be multiplied, and the years of your life shall be increased.   PROVERBS 9:11

The fear of the LORD prolongs days: but the years of the wicked shall be shortened.   PROVERBS 10:27

He has made every thing beautiful in His time: also He has set the world in their heart, so that no man can find out the work that God makes from the beginning to the end. I know that there is no good in them, but for a man to rejoice, and to do good in his life. And also that every man should eat and drink, and enjoy the good of all his labor, it is the gift of God.   ECCLESIASTES 3:11–13

I beseech you therefore, brethren, by the mercies of God, that you present your bodies a living sacrifice, holy, acceptable to God, which is your reasonable service. And be not conformed to this world: but be you transformed by the renewing of your mind, that you may prove what is that good, and acceptable, and perfect, will of God. ROMANS 12:1–2

Therefore if any man be in Christ, he is a new creature: old things are passed away; behold, all things are become new. 2 CORINTHIANS 5:17

That you put off concerning the former conversation the old man, which is corrupt according to the deceitful lusts; and be renewed in the spirit of your mind; and that you put on the new man, which after God is created in righteousness and true holiness. EPHESIANS 4:22–24

Be careful for nothing; but in every thing by prayer and supplication with thanksgiving let your requests be made known to God. And the peace of God, which passes all understanding, shall keep your hearts and minds through Christ Jesus. PHILIPPIANS 4:6–7

He that overcomes shall inherit all things; and I will be his God, and he shall be My son. REVELATION 21:7

CHARACTER

And you shall love the LORD your God with all your heart, and with all your soul, and with all your might. And these words, which I command you this day, shall be in your heart.

DEUTERONOMY 6:5–6

Beware that you forget not the LORD your God, in not keeping His commandments, and His judgments, and His statutes, which I command you this day.　　　　DEUTERONOMY 8:11

Behold, I set before you this day a blessing and a curse; a blessing, if you obey the commandments of the LORD your God, which I command you this day: and a curse, if you will not obey the commandments of the LORD your God, but turn aside out of the way which I command you this day, to go after other gods, which you have not known.　　　　DEUTERONOMY 11:26–28

Therefore all things whatsoever you would that men should do to you, do you even so to them: for this is the law and the prophets.

MATTHEW 7:12

Likewise, you younger, submit yourselves to the elder. Yea, all of you be subject one to another, and be clothed with humility: for God resists the proud, and gives grace to the humble.

1 PETER 5:5

INSIGHTS ON FAITH FROM SMITH WIGGLESWORTH

Oh, brothers and sisters, I want you to see that that power is yours. God is delighted when we use the power He has given us.

✎

How can we get more faith? God's Word tells us, *"Faith comes by hearing, and hearing by the word of God"* (Rom. 10:17). Faith is a gift. We receive our inheritance by faith. We are spiritual children—*"children of God without fault"* (Phil. 2:15). May God manifest this in us by the power of His might.

✎

God has not promised that as Christians we will always feel very wonderful, but He has promised that if we stand on His Word, He will make His Word real in our lives. First we exercise faith; then it becomes fact.

✎

All things are possible for us in God.

COMMITMENT

If a man vow a vow to the LORD, or swear an oath to bind his soul with a bond; he shall not break his word, he shall do according to all that proceeds out of his mouth. NUMBERS 30:2

Commit your way to the LORD; trust also in Him; and He shall bring it to pass. PSALM 37:5

But let your communication be, Yea, yea; Nay, nay: for whatsoever is more than these comes of evil. MATTHEW 5:37

If a man abide not in Me, he is cast forth as a branch, and is withered; and men gather them, and cast them into the fire, and they are burned. If you abide in Me, and My words abide in you, you shall ask what you will, and it shall be done to you.

JOHN 15:6–7

Therefore, my beloved brethren, be you steadfast, unmovable, always abounding in the work of the Lord, forasmuch as you know that your labor is not in vain in the Lord.

1 CORINTHIANS 15:58

CONFESSION

Whosoever therefore shall confess Me before men, him will I confess also before My Father which is in heaven. But whosoever shall deny Me before men, him will I also deny before My Father which is in heaven.　　　　　　　　　　　　　　MATTHEW 10:32–33

Also I say to you, Whosoever shall confess Me before men, him shall the Son of man also confess before the angels of God.

LUKE 12:8

That if you shall confess with your mouth the Lord Jesus, and shall believe in your heart that God has raised Him from the dead, you shall be saved. For with the heart man believes to righteousness; and with the mouth confession is made to salvation.

ROMANS 10:9–10

Wherefore God also has highly exalted Him, and given Him a name which is above every name: that at the name of Jesus every knee should bow, of things in heaven, and things in earth, and things under the earth; and that every tongue should confess that Jesus Christ is Lord, to the glory of God the Father.

PHILIPPIANS 2:9–11

And every spirit that confesses not that Jesus Christ is come in the flesh is not of God: and this is that spirit of antichrist, whereof you have heard that it should come; and even now already is it in the world.　　　　　　　　　　　　　　　　　1 JOHN 4:3

CONTENTMENT

You will keep him in perfect peace, whose mind is stayed on You: because he trusts in You. ISAIAH 26:3

A little that a righteous man has is better than the riches of many wicked. For the arms of the wicked shall be broken: but the LORD upholds the righteous. PSALM 37:16–17

He will fulfill the desire of them that fear Him: He also will hear their cry, and will save them. PSALM 145:19

The backslider in heart shall be filled with his own ways: and a good man shall be satisfied from himself. PROVERBS 14:14

A sound heart is the life of the flesh: but envy the rottenness of the bones. PROVERBS 14:30

All the days of the afflicted are evil: but he that is of a merry heart has a continual feast. PROVERBS 15:15

Better is the poor that walks in his uprightness, than he that is perverse in his ways, though he be rich. PROVERBS 28:6

A faithful man shall abound with blessings: but he that makes haste to be rich shall not be innocent. PROVERBS 28:20

INSIGHTS ON FAITH FROM SMITH WIGGLESWORTH

It is possible for you to be in a place where God is pouring out His Spirit and yet miss the blessing that God is so willing to bestow. This is all due to a lack of revelation and a misunderstanding of the infinite grace of God and of *"the God of all grace"* (1 Pet. 5:10), who is willing to give to all who will reach out the hand of faith. This life that He freely bestows is a gift. Some think they have to earn it, and they miss the whole thing. Oh, for a simple faith to receive all that God so lavishly offers!

~

I want to tell you that you can please God and get things from God only through a living faith. God never fails. God never can fail.

~

The purpose of God for us is that we might be on the earth for a manifestation of His glory, that every time satanic power is confronted, God might be able to say of us as He did of Job, "What do you think about him?" (See Job 1:8.) God wants us so manifested in His divine plan in the earth that Satan will have to hear God.

CONTENTMENT

Therefore I says to you, Take no thought for your life, what you shall eat, or what you shall drink; nor yet for your body, what you shall put on. Is not the life more than meat, and the body than raiment? Behold the fowls of the air: for they sow not, neither do they reap, nor gather into barns; yet your heavenly Father feeds them. Are you not much better than they? MATTHEW 6:25–26

But seek you first the kingdom of God, and His righteousness; and all these things shall be added to you. MATTHEW 6:33

Therefore I take pleasure in infirmities, in reproaches, in necessities, in persecutions, in distresses for Christ's sake: for when I am weak, then am I strong. 2 CORINTHIANS 12:10

Not that I speak in respect of want: for I have learned, in whatsoever state I am, therewith to be content. I know both how to be abased, and I know how to abound: every where and in all things I am instructed both to be full and to be hungry, both to abound and to suffer need. PHILIPPIANS 4:11–12

But my God shall supply all your need according to His riches in glory by Christ Jesus. PHILIPPIANS 4:19

Let your conversation be without covetousness; and be content with such things as you have: for He has said, I will never leave you, nor forsake you. HEBREWS 13:5

DECEIT

The heart is deceitful above all things, and desperately wicked: who can know it? I the Lord *search the heart, I try the reins, even to give every man according to his ways, and according to the fruit of his doings.*   Jeremiah 17:9–10

He that works deceit shall not dwell within My house: he that tells lies shall not tarry in My sight.   Psalm 101:7

Bread of deceit is sweet to a man; but afterwards his mouth shall be filled with gravel.   Proverbs 20:17

Favor is deceitful, and beauty is vain: but a woman that fears the Lord, *she shall be praised.*   Proverbs 31:30

Beware lest any man spoil you through philosophy and vain deceit, after the tradition of men, after the rudiments of the world, and not after Christ.   Colossians 2:8

But exhort one another daily, while it is called Today; lest any of you be hardened through the deceitfulness of sin.

Hebrews 3:13

DISCIPLESHIP

Iron sharpens iron; so a man sharpens the countenance of his friend.　　　　　　　　　　　　　　　PROVERBS 27:17

Therefore whosoever hears these sayings of Mine, and does them, I will liken him to a wise man, which built his house upon a rock: and the rain descended, and the floods came, and the winds blew, and beat upon that house; and it fell not: for it was founded upon a rock.　　　　　　　　　　　　　　MATTHEW 7:24–25

And when he puts forth his own sheep, he goes before them, and the sheep follow him: for they know his voice.　　　JOHN 10:4

By this shall all men know that you are My disciples, if you have love one to another.　　　　　　　　　　　JOHN 13:35

But you shall receive power, after that the Holy Ghost is come upon you: and you shall be witnesses to Me both in Jerusalem, and in all Judaea, and in Samaria, and to the uttermost part of the earth.　　　　　　　　　　　　　　　ACTS 1:8

For the grace of God that brings salvation has appeared to all men, teaching us that, denying ungodliness and worldly lusts, we should live soberly, righteously, and godly, in this present world.　　　　　　　　　　　　　　　TITUS 2:11–12

INSIGHTS ON FAITH FROM SMITH WIGGLESWORTH

We will never know the mind of God until we learn to know the voice of God.

⌒

But praise God, He is the truth; He is the life; and His Word is Spirit and life-giving. And when we understand it in its true order to us, we find that it is not only the Word of life, but it quickens, opens, fills, moves, changes, and brings us into a place where we dare to say, "Amen!"

⌒

Do not forget, the Holy Ghost did not come as a cleanser. The Holy Ghost is not a cleanser. The Holy Ghost is a revealer of imperfection, which takes the blood of Jesus to cleanse. After the blood has cleansed the imperfection, you need the Word of God, for the Word of God is the only power which creates anew. Life comes through the Word. The Word is the Son. He that has received the Son has received life; he that has not received the Son has not life.

GOALS

And it shall come to pass, if you shall hearken diligently to the voice of the Lord your God, to observe and to do all His commandments which I command you this day, that the Lord your God will set you on high above all nations of the earth: and all these blessings shall come on you, and overtake you, if you shall hearken unto the voice of the Lord your God.

Deuteronomy 28:1–2

Delight yourself also in the Lord: and He shall give you the desires of your heart. Commit your way to the Lord; trust also in Him; and He shall bring it to pass. Psalm 37:4–5

Know you not that they which run in a race run all, but one receives the prize? So run, that you may obtain. And every man that strives for the mastery is temperate in all things. Now they do it to obtain a corruptible crown; but we an incorruptible.

1 Corinthians 9:24–25

Brethren, I count not myself to have apprehended: but this one thing I do, forgetting those things which are behind, and reaching forth to those things which are before, I press toward the mark for the prize of the high calling of God in Christ Jesus.

Philippians 3:13–14

And let us not be weary in well doing: for in due season we shall reap, if we faint not. Galatians 6:9

INSIGHTS ON FAITH FROM SMITH WIGGLESWORTH

How great our faith should be, for we cannot be saved except by faith. We cannot be kept except by faith. We can only be baptized by faith, and we will be caught up by faith; therefore, what a blessed reality is faith in the living God.

⌒

Believe that when you come into the presence of God you can have all you came for. You can take it away, and you can use it, for all the power of God is at your disposal in response to your faith.

⌒

Faith is the Word of God. It is the personal inward flow of divine favor, which moves in every fiber of our being until our whole nature is so quickened that we live by faith, we move by faith, and we are going to be caught up to glory by faith, for faith is the victory!

MERCY

And David said to Gad, I am in a great strait: let us fall now into the hand of the LORD; for His mercies are great: and let me not fall into the hand of man. 2 SAMUEL 24:14

Come now, and let us reason together, says the LORD: though your sins be as scarlet, they shall be as white as snow; though they be red like crimson, they shall be as wool. ISAIAH 1:18

And therefore will the LORD wait, that He may be gracious to you, and therefore will He be exalted, that He may have mercy upon you: for the LORD is a God of judgment: blessed are all they that wait for Him. ISAIAH 30:18

For My name's sake will I defer My anger, and for My praise will I refrain for you, that I cut you not off. ISAIAH 48:9

In all their affliction He was afflicted, and the angel of His presence saved them: in His love and in His pity He redeemed them; and He bore them, and carried them all the days of old.
ISAIAH 63:9

But the mercy of the LORD is from everlasting to everlasting upon them that fear Him, and His righteousness to children's children. PSALM 103:17

Hear my prayer, O Lord, give ear to my supplications: in Your faithfulness answer me, and in Your righteousness.

PSALM 143:1

Blessed are the merciful: for they shall obtain mercy.

MATTHEW 5:7

Be you therefore merciful, as your Father also is merciful.

LUKE 6:36

And he said to me, My grace is sufficient for you: for my strength is made perfect in weakness. Most gladly therefore will I rather glory in my infirmities, that the power of Christ may rest upon me. Therefore I take pleasure in infirmities, in reproaches, in necessities, in persecutions, in distresses for Christ's sake: for when I am weak, then am I strong.   2 CORINTHIANS 12:9–10

As we have therefore opportunity, let us do good to all men, especially to them who are of the household of faith.

GALATIANS 6:10

But God, who is rich in mercy, for His great love wherewith He loved us, even when we were dead in sins, has quickened us together with Christ, by grace you are saved.

EPHESIANS 2:4–5

Put on therefore, as the elect of God, holy and beloved, bowels of
mercies, kindness, humbleness of mind, meekness, longsuffering.

COLOSSIANS 3:12

Let us therefore come boldly to the throne of grace, that we may
obtain mercy, and find grace to help in time of need.

HEBREWS 4:16

Finally, be you all of one mind, having compassion one of another,
love as brethren, be pitiful, be courteous: not rendering evil for
evil, or railing for railing: but contrariwise blessing; knowing that
you are thereto called, that you should inherit a blessing.

1 PETER 3:8–9

And beside this, giving all diligence, add to your faith virtue;
and to virtue knowledge; and to knowledge temperance; and to
temperance patience; and to patience godliness; and to godliness
brotherly kindness; and to brotherly kindness charity. For if these
things be in you, and abound, they make you that you shall nei-
ther be barren nor unfruitful in the knowledge of our Lord Jesus
Christ.

2 PETER 1:5–8

Mercy to you, and peace, and love, be multiplied.

JUDE 2

TRUST

I will instruct you and teach you in the way which you shall go: I will guide you with My eye.   PSALM 32:8

Trust in the LORD with all your heart; and lean not to your own understanding. In all your ways acknowledge Him, and He shall direct your paths. Be not wise in your own eyes: fear the LORD, and depart from evil. It shall be health to your navel, and marrow to your bones.   PROVERBS 3:5–8

Fear you not; for I am with you: be not dismayed; for I am Your God: I will strengthen you; yea, I will help you; yea, I will uphold you with the right hand of My righteousness.   ISAIAH 41:10

For the vision is yet for an appointed time, but at the end it shall speak, and not lie: though it tarry, wait for it; because it will surely come, it will not tarry.   HABAKKUK 2:3

And He says to them, Why are you fearful, O you of little faith? Then He arose, and rebuked the winds and the sea; and there was a great calm.   MATTHEW 8:26

Jesus answered and said to them, Verily I say unto you, If you have faith, and doubt not, you shall not only do this which is done to the fig tree, but also if you shall say to this mountain, Be you removed, and be you cast into the sea; it shall be done.

MATTHEW 21:21

For verily I say to you, That whosoever shall say to this mountain, Be you removed, and be you cast into the sea; and shall not doubt in his heart, but shall believe that those things which he says shall come to pass; he shall have whatsoever he says.   MARK 11:23

And he that doubts is damned if he eat, because he eats not of faith: for whatsoever is not of faith is sin.   ROMANS 14:23

Wherefore seeing we also are compassed about with so great a cloud of witnesses, let us lay aside every weight, and the sin which does so easily beset us, and let us run with patience the race that is set before us, looking to Jesus the author and finisher of our faith; who for the joy that was set before Him endured the cross, despising the shame, and is set down at the right hand of the throne of God.   HEBREWS 12:1–2

And the Lord direct your hearts into the love of God, and into the patient waiting for Christ.   2 THESSALONIANS 3:5

INSIGHTS ON FAITH FROM SMITH WIGGLESWORTH

"Faith is the glorious knowledge of a personal presence within you, changing you from strength to strength, from glory to glory, until you get to the place where you walk with God, and God thinks and speaks through you by the power of the Holy Spirit. Oh, it is grand; it is glorious!

⌒

What will happen if we really open the door by faith? God is greater than our thoughts. He puts it to us, "*exceedingly abundantly above all that we ask or think*" (Eph. 3:20). When we ask a lot, God says "more." Are we ready for the "more"? And then the "much more"? We must be, or we will miss it.

⌒

Don't stumble at the Word. If Jesus says anything, if the Word conveys anything to your mind, don't stumble at the Word. Believe that God is greater than you are, greater than your heart, greater than your thought, and that He can establish you in righteousness even when your thoughts and your knowledge are absolutely against it. He blotted out our transgressions in a thick cloud, and our sins, our iniquities, will He remember no more forever.

"WHEN THERE IS A STANDARD THAT HAS NOT YET BEEN REACHED IN YOUR LIFE, GOD BY HIS GRACE, BY HIS MERCY, AND BY YOUR YIELDEDNESS CAN FIT YOU FOR THAT PLACE. YOU CAN NEVER BE PREPARED FOR IT EXCEPT BY A BROKEN HEART AND A CONTRITE SPIRIT, AND BY YIELDING TO THE WILL OF GOD. BUT IF YOU WILL COME WITH A WHOLE HEART TO THE THRONE OF GRACE, GOD WILL MEET YOU AND BUILD YOU UP ON HIS SPIRITUAL PLANE."

—SMITH WIGGLESWORTH

6

THE WAY OF FAITH

ASSURANCE

And the fear of the LORD fell upon all the kingdoms of the lands that were round about Judah, so that they made no war against Jehoshaphat. 2 CHRONICLES 17:10

God is our refuge and strength, a very present help in trouble. PSALM 46:1

He shall not be afraid of evil tidings: his heart is fixed, trusting in the LORD. PSALM 112:7

In all your ways acknowledge Him, and He shall direct your paths. PROVERBS 3:6

For the mountains shall depart, and the hills be removed; but My kindness shall not depart from you, neither shall the covenant of My peace be removed, says the LORD that has mercy on you. ISAIAH 54:10

Blessed are the pure in heart: for they shall see God.

MATTHEW 5:8

And He said to them, Why are you so fearful? how is it that you have no faith? MARK 4:40

And immediately the father of the child cried out, and said with tears, Lord, I believe; help You my unbelief. MARK 9:24

And he answering said, You shall love the Lord your God with all your heart, and with all your soul, and with all your strength, and with all your mind; and your neighbor as yourself. LUKE 10:27

And the apostles said to the Lord, Increase our faith. LUKE 17:5

In the beginning was the Word, and the Word was with God, and the Word was God. JOHN 1:1

He that believes on the Son has everlasting life: and he that believes not the Son shall not see life; but the wrath of God abides on him. JOHN 3:36

But the Comforter, which is the Holy Ghost, whom the Father will send in My name, He shall teach you all things, and bring all things to your remembrance, whatsoever I have said to you.

JOHN 14:26

Peace I leave with you, My peace I give to you: not as the world gives, give I to you. Let not your heart be troubled, neither let it be afraid.   JOHN 14:27

And they said, Believe on the Lord Jesus Christ, and you shall be saved, and your house.   ACTS 16:31

And we know that all things work together for good to them that love God, to them who are the called according to His purpose.
                                             ROMANS 8:28

And he that doubts is damned if he eat, because he eats not of faith: for whatsoever is not of faith is sin.   ROMANS 14:23

And now abides faith, hope, charity, these three; but the greatest of these is charity.   1 CORINTHIANS 13:13

For by grace are you saved through faith; and that not of yourselves: it is the gift of God: not of works, lest any man should boast.   EPHESIANS 2:8–9

INSIGHTS ON FAITH FROM SMITH WIGGLESWORTH

What it means for people to have faith! What it will mean when we all have faith! We know that as soon as faith is in perfect operation, we will be in the perfect place where God is manifested right before our eyes. The pure in heart will see God, and all the steps of purity are a divine appointment of more faith. The more purity, the more faith.

I tell you, God can arrange everything. He can plan for you, and when He plans for you, all is peace. All things are possible if you will believe.

Faith has it. Faith claims it because it has got it. *"Faith is the substance of things hoped for, the evidence of things not seen"* (Hebrews 11:1). As sure as you have faith, God will give you grace overflowing, and when He comes in, you will speak as the Spirit giveth utterance.

ASSURANCE

According to the eternal purpose which He purposed in Christ Jesus our Lord: in whom we have boldness and access with confidence by the faith of Him.   EPHESIANS 3:11–12

That you put off concerning the former conversation the old man, which is corrupt according to the deceitful lusts; and be renewed in the spirit of your mind; and that you put on the new man, which after God is created in righteousness and true holiness.
                                                    EPHESIANS 4:22–24

Jesus Christ the same yesterday, and to day, and for ever.
                                                    HEBREWS 13:8

By Him therefore let us offer the sacrifice of praise to God continually, that is, the fruit of our lips giving thanks to His name.
                                                    HEBREWS 13:15

For we have not an high priest which cannot be touched with the feeling of our infirmities; but was in all points tempted like as we are, yet without sin. Let us therefore come boldly to the throne of grace, that we may obtain mercy, and find grace to help in time of need.   HEBREWS 4:15–16

CONTROL OVER SIN

For their redeemer is mighty; He shall plead their cause with you.   PROVERBS 23:11

And I will feed them that oppress you with their own flesh; and they shall be drunken with their own blood, as with sweet wine: and all flesh shall know that I the LORD am your Saviour and your Redeemer, the mighty One of Jacob.   ISAIAH 49:26

For sin shall not have dominion over you: for you are not under the law, but under grace.   ROMANS 6:14

Christ has redeemed us from the curse of the law, being made a curse for us: for it is written, Cursed is every one that hangs on a tree.   GALATIANS 3:13

But if we walk in the light, as He is in the light, we have fellowship one with another, and the blood of Jesus Christ His Son cleanses us from all sin.   1 JOHN 1:7

CONTROL OVER TEMPTATION

That your faith should not stand in the wisdom of men, but in the power of God.   1 CORINTHIANS 2:5

Flee fornication. Every sin that a man does is without the body; but he that commits fornication sins against his own body.
                                                      1 CORINTHIANS 6:18

There has no temptation taken you but such as is common to man: but God is faithful, who will not suffer you to be tempted above that you are able; but will with the temptation also make a way to escape, that you may be able to bear it.
                                                     1 CORINTHIANS 10:13

Holding faith, and a good conscience; which some having put away concerning faith have made shipwreck.   1 TIMOTHY 1:19

Wherein you greatly rejoice, though now for a season, if need be, you are in heaviness through manifold temptations: that the trial of your faith, being much more precious than of gold that perishes, though it be tried with fire, might be found to praise and honor and glory at the appearing of Jesus Christ: whom having not seen, you love; in whom, though now you see Him not, yet believing, you rejoice with joy unspeakable and full of glory: receiving the end of your faith, even the salvation of your souls.
                                                          1 PETER 1:6–9

INSIGHTS ON FAITH FROM SMITH WIGGLESWORTH

God wants to establish our faith so that we will grasp this divine life, this divine nature of the Son of God, in order that our *"spirit, soul, and body* [will] *be* [sanctified completely and] *preserved blameless at the coming of our Lord Jesus Christ"* (1 Thess. 5:23).

◡

Oh, thank God for His Word! Live it. Be moved by His Word. We will become flat and anemic and helpless without this Word. You are not any good for anything apart from the Word. The Word is everything; the Word has to become everything. When the heavens and the earth are melted away, then we will be as bright as, and brighter than, the day because of the Word of God.

◡

God can never bless us when we are being hard-hearted, critical, or unforgiving. These things will hinder faith quicker than anything.

DEPENDENCE

Though I walk in the midst of trouble, You will revive me: You shall stretch forth Your hand against the wrath of my enemies, and Your right hand shall save me. The LORD will perfect that which concerns me: Your mercy, O LORD, endures for ever: forsake not the works of Your own hands.　　　PSALM 138:7–8

Every way of a man is right in his own eyes: but the LORD ponders the hearts. To do justice and judgment is more acceptable to the LORD than sacrifice.　　　PROVERBS 21:2–3

And I will make an everlasting covenant with them, that I will not turn away from them, to do them good; but I will put My fear in their hearts, that they shall not depart from me.

JEREMIAH 32:40

Call to Me, and I will answer you, and show you great and mighty things, which you know not.　　　JEREMIAH 33:3

Then shall we know, if we follow on to know the LORD: His going forth is prepared as the morning; and He shall come to us as the rain, as the latter and former rain to the earth.　　　HOSEA 6:3

Come to Me, all you that labor and are heavy laden, and I will give you rest. Take My yoke upon you, and learn of Me; for I am meek and lowly in heart: and you shall find rest to your souls.

MATTHEW 11:28–29

What shall we then say to these things? If God be for us, who can be against us? He that spared not His own Son, but delivered Him up for us all, how shall He not with Him also freely give us all things?　　　　　　　　　　　　　　Romans 8:31–32

Let us hold fast the profession of our faith without wavering; for He is faithful that promised.　　　　　　　　Hebrews 10:23

Wherefore seeing we also are compassed about with so great a cloud of witnesses, let us lay aside every weight, and the sin which does so easily beset us, and let us run with patience the race that is set before us, looking to Jesus the author and finisher of our faith; who for the joy that was set before Him endured the cross, despising the shame, and is set down at the right hand of the throne of God. For consider Him that endured such contradiction of sinners against Himself, lest you be wearied and faint in your minds.　　　　　　　　　　　　　　Hebrews 12:1–3

FUTURE

A man's heart devises his way: but the LORD directs his steps.

PROVERBS 16:9

Let not your heart envy sinners: but be you in the fear of the LORD all the day long. For surely there is an end; and your expectation shall not be cut off. PROVERBS 23:17–18

And there is hope in your end, says the LORD, that your children shall come again to their own border. JEREMIAH 31:17

In My Father's house are many mansions: if it were not so, I would have told you. I go to prepare a place for you. And if I go and prepare a place for you, I will come again, and receive you to Myself; that where I am, there you may be also. JOHN 14:2–3

These things I have spoken to you, that in Me you might have peace. In the world you shall have tribulation: but be of good cheer; I have overcome the world. JOHN 16:33

INSIGHTS ON FAITH FROM SMITH WIGGLESWORTH

No person who has Jesus as the inward power of his body needs to be trembling when Satan comes around. All he has to do is to stand still and see the salvation of the Lord.

⌒

If you turn to 2 Peter 1:4, you will find that we have received His divine nature, which is infinite power, infinite knowledge, infinite pleasure, and infinite revelation. People are missing it because we have failed to apply it. But God is making up a people who will have to be firstfruits. By simple faith, you entered in and claimed your rights and became Christians, being born again because you believed.

⌒

What is faith? Faith is the living principle of the Word of God. It is life; it produces life; it changes life.

GIVING

*Honor the L*ORD *with your substance, and with the firstfruits of all your increase: So shall your barns be filled with plenty, and your presses shall burst out with new wine.*   PROVERBS 3:9–10

Withhold not good from them to whom it is due, when it is in the power of your hand to do it.   PROVERBS 3:27

The liberal soul shall be made fat: and he that waters shall be watered also himself.   PROVERBS 11:25

He covets greedily all the day long: but the righteous gives and spares not.   PROVERBS 21:26

*Bring you all the tithes into the storehouse, that there may be meat in My house, and prove Me now herewith, says the L*ORD *of hosts, if I will not open you the windows of heaven, and pour you out a blessing, that there shall not be room enough to receive it. And I will rebuke the devourer for your sakes, and he shall not destroy the fruits of your ground; neither shall your vine cast her fruit before the time in the field, says the L*ORD *of hosts.*   MALACHI 3:10–11

Heal the sick, cleanse the lepers, raise the dead, cast out devils: freely you have received, freely give.   MATTHEW 10:8

And whosoever shall give to drink to one of these little ones a cup of cold water only in the name of a disciple, verily I say to you, he shall in no wise lose his reward.   MATTHEW 10:42

Give, and it shall be given to you; good measure, pressed down, and shaken together, and running over, shall men give into your bosom. For with the same measure that you mete withal it shall be measured to you again.   LUKE 6:38

I have showed you all things, how that so laboring you ought to support the weak, and to remember the words of the Lord Jesus, how He said, It is more blessed to give than to receive.

ACTS 20:35

Every man according as he purposed in his heart, so let him give; not grudgingly, or of necessity: for God loves a cheerful giver.

2 CORINTHIANS 9:7

HEAVEN

The heavens declare the glory of God; and the firmament shows His handiwork.   PSALM 19:1

And Jesus said to him, Verily I say to you, Today shall you be with Me in paradise.   LUKE 23:43

In My Father's house are many mansions: if it were not so, I would have told you. I go to prepare a place for you. And if I go and prepare a place for you, I will come again, and receive you to Myself; that where I am, there you may be also.   JOHN 14:2–3

But as it is written, Eye has not seen, nor ear heard, neither have entered into the heart of man, the things which God has prepared for them that love Him.   1 CORINTHIANS 2:9

For Christ is not entered into the holy places made with hands, which are the figures of the true; but into heaven itself, now to appear in the presence of God for us.   HEBREWS 9:24

But you are come to mount Zion, and to the city of the living God, the heavenly Jerusalem, and to an innumerable company of angels.   HEBREWS 12:22

INSIGHTS ON FAITH FROM SMITH WIGGLESWORTH

I am looking forward to and believing the fact that He is coming again. And this hope in me brings me to the same place as the man of faith who looked for a city that human hands have not made. There is a city that human hands have not made, and by faith we have a right to claim our position right along as we go.

⌒

Whatever God has done in the past, His name is still the same. When hearts are burdened and they come face to face with the need of the day, they look into God's Word, and it brings in a propeller of power or an anointing that makes them know that He has truly visited.

⌒

When you have faith in Christ, the love of God is so real that you feel you could do anything for Jesus. Whoever believes, loves. "We love Him because He first loved us" (1 John 4:19). When did He love us? When we were in the mire. What did He say? "Your sins are forgiven you" (Luke 5:20). Why did He say it? Because He loved us. What for? That He might bring many sons into glory. What was His purpose? That we might be with Him forever.

HOPE

Be of good courage, and He shall strengthen your heart, all you that hope in the LORD.   PSALM 31:24

Let Your mercy, O LORD, be upon us, according as we hope in You.   PSALM 33:22

Why are you cast down, O my soul? and why are you disquieted within me? hope in God: for I shall yet praise Him, who is the health of my countenance, and my God.   PSALM 43:5

For You are my hope, O LORD God: You are my trust from my youth.   PSALM 71:5

Uphold me according to Your word, that I may live: and let me not be ashamed of my hope.   PSALM 119:116

For whom the LORD loves He corrects; even as a father the son in whom he delights.   PROVERBS 3:12

Blessed is the man that trusts in the LORD, and whose hope the LORD is. For he shall be as a tree planted by the waters, and that spreads out her roots by the river, and shall not see when heat comes, but her leaf shall be green; and shall not be careful in the year of drought, neither shall cease from yielding fruit.

JEREMIAH 17:7–8

But they that wait upon the LORD shall renew their strength; they shall mount up with wings as eagles; they shall run, and not be weary; and they shall walk, and not faint.　　　ISAIAH 40:31

The LORD is my portion, says my soul; therefore will I hope in Him. The LORD is good to them that wait for Him, to the soul that seeks Him.　　　LAMENTATIONS 3:24–25

O death, where is your sting? O grave, where is your victory? The sting of death is sin; and the strength of sin is the law. But thanks be to God, which gives us the victory through our Lord Jesus Christ. Therefore, my beloved brethren, be you steadfast, unmovable, always abounding in the work of the Lord, forasmuch as you know that your labor is not in vain in the Lord.

1 CORINTHIANS 15:55–58

Now to Him that is able to do exceeding abundantly above all that we ask or think, according to the power that works in us, to Him be glory in the church by Christ Jesus throughout all ages, world without end. Amen.　　　EPHESIANS 3:20–21

To whom God would make known what is the riches of the glory of this mystery among the Gentiles; which is Christ in you, the hope of glory.　　　COLOSSIANS 1:27

Remembering without ceasing your work of faith, and labor of love, and patience of hope in our Lord Jesus Christ, in the sight of God and our Father.　　　　　1 THESSALONIANS 1:3

For I am persuaded, that neither death, nor life, nor angels, nor principalities, nor powers, nor things present, nor things to come, nor height, nor depth, nor any other creature, shall be able to separate us from the love of God, which is in Christ Jesus our Lord.　　　　　ROMANS 8:38–39

Now faith is the substance of things hoped for, the evidence of things not seen.　　　　　HEBREWS 11:1

Wherefore gird up the loins of your mind, be sober, and hope to the end for the grace that is to be brought to you at the revelation of Jesus Christ.　　　　　1 PETER 1:13

Who by Him do believe in God, that raised Him up from the dead, and gave Him glory; that your faith and hope might be in God.　　　　　1 PETER 1:21

Casting all your care upon Him; for He cares for you.　　　　　1 PETER 5:7

And every man that has this hope in Him purifies himself, even as He is pure.　　　　　1 JOHN 3:3

INSIGHTS ON FAITH FROM SMITH WIGGLESWORTH

God wants manifestation, and He wants His glory to be seen. He wants us all to be filled with the thought that He can look upon us and delight in us subduing the world unto Him. You are going to miss a great deal if you don't begin to act. But once you begin to act in the order of God, you will find that God establishes your faith and from that day starts you along the line of the promises.

⌇

You cannot find anywhere that God ever failed. And He wants to bring us into that blessed place of faith, changing us into a real substance of faith, until we are so like-minded that whatever we ask, we believe we receive, and our joy becomes full because we believe.

⌇

It is all divine order. There is nothing wrong in the plan of God. It is all in perfect order. To think that God can make a mistake is the biggest blunder that a man makes in his life. God makes no mistakes. But when we are in the will of God, the plan works out admirably because it is divine and thought out by the almightiness of God.

WALKING WITH GOD

Commit your way to the LORD; trust also in Him; and He shall bring it to pass. And He shall bring forth your righteousness as the light, and your judgment as the noonday. PSALM 37:5–6

The LORD is my shepherd; I shall not want. He makes me to lie down in green pastures: He leads me beside the still waters. He restores my soul: He leads me in the paths of righteousness for His name's sake. Yea, though I walk through the valley of the shadow of death, I will fear no evil: for You are with me; Your rod and Your staff they comfort me. You prepare a table before me in the presence of my enemies: You anoint my head with oil; my cup runs over. Surely goodness and mercy shall follow me all the days of my life: and I will dwell in the house of the LORD for ever. PSALM 23

Trust in the LORD with all your heart; and lean not to your own understanding. In all your ways acknowledge Him, and He shall direct your paths. PROVERBS 3:5–6

For I know the thoughts that I think toward you, says the LORD, thoughts of peace, and not of evil, to give you an expected end. JEREMIAH 29:11

*Therefore you shall keep the commandments of the L*ORD *your God to walk in His ways, and to fear Him.*

DEUTERONOMY 8:6

You have heard that it has been said, An eye for an eye, and a tooth for a tooth: but I say to you, That you resist not evil: but whosoever shall smite you on your right cheek, turn to him the other also.   MATTHEW 5:38–39

No man can serve two masters: for either he will hate the one, and love the other; or else he will hold to the one, and despise the other. You cannot serve God and mammon.   MATTHEW 6:24

And Jesus answering says to them, Have faith in God. For verily I say to you, That whosoever shall say to this mountain, Be you removed, and be you cast into the sea; and shall not doubt in his heart, but shall believe that those things which he says shall come to pass; he shall have whatsoever he says. Therefore I say to you, What things soever you desire, when you pray, believe that you receive them, and you shall have them.

MARK 11:22–24

I tell you, Nay: but, except you repent, you shall all likewise perish.   LUKE 13:3

Jesus answered and said to them, This is the work of God, that you believe on Him whom He has sent. JOHN 6:29

Verily, verily, I say to you, He that believes on Me has everlasting life. JOHN 6:47

I said therefore to you, that you shall die in your sins: for if you believe not that I am He, you shall die in your sins. JOHN 8:24

Verily, verily, I say to you, He that believes on Me, the works that I do shall he do also; and greater works than these shall he do; because I go to My Father. And whatsoever you shall ask in My name, that will I do, that the Father may be glorified in the Son. If you shall ask any thing in My name, I will do it.

JOHN 14:12–14

Then went this saying abroad among the brethren, that that disciple should not die: yet Jesus said not to him, He shall not die; but, If I will that he tarry till I come, what is that to you?

JOHN 21:23

INSIGHTS ON FAITH FROM SMITH WIGGLESWORTH

I am as confident as possible that if we could get to the place of believing God, we would not need to rely on a dog in the yard or a lock on the door. All this is unbelief. God is able to manage the whole business. It doesn't matter how many thieves are about; they cannot break through or steal where God is.

∽

A man full of faith hopes against hope. He shouts while the walls are up, and they come down while he shouts. God has this faith for us in Christ. We must be careful that no unbelief and no wavering are found in us.

∽

There is nothing impossible with God. All the impossibility is with us when we measure God by the limitations of our unbelief. We have a wonderful God, a God whose ways are past finding out and whose grace and power are limitless.

WALKING WITH GOD

Then Peter said to them, Repent, and be baptized every one of you in the name of Jesus Christ for the remission of sins, and you shall receive the gift of the Holy Ghost.   ACTS 2:38

He staggered not at the promise of God through unbelief; but was strong in faith, giving glory to God.   ROMANS 4:20

Therefore being justified by faith, we have peace with God through our Lord Jesus Christ: by whom also we have access by faith into this grace wherein we stand, and rejoice in hope of the glory of God. And not only so, but we glory in tribulations also: knowing that tribulation works patience; and patience, experience; and experience, hope: and hope makes not ashamed; because the love of God is shed abroad in our hearts by the Holy Ghost which is given to us.   ROMANS 5:1–5

For I say, through the grace given to me, to every man that is among you, not to think of himself more highly than he ought to think; but to think soberly, according as God has dealt to every man the measure of faith.   ROMANS 12:3

For we walk by faith, not by sight.   2 CORINTHIANS 5:7

I am crucified with Christ: nevertheless I live; yet not I, but Christ lives in me: and the life which I now live in the flesh I live by the faith of the Son of God, who loved me, and gave Himself for me.

GALATIANS 2:20

For you are all the children of God by faith in Christ Jesus. For as many of you as have been baptized into Christ have put on Christ.

GALATIANS 3:26–27

That Christ may dwell in your hearts by faith; that you, being rooted and grounded in love, may be able to comprehend with all saints what is the breadth, and length, and depth, and height; and to know the love of Christ, which passes knowledge, that you might be filled with all the fullness of God.

EPHESIANS 3:17–19

I can do all things through Christ which strengthens me.

PHILIPPIANS 4:13

As you have therefore received Christ Jesus the Lord, so walk you in Him: rooted and built up in Him, and established in the faith, as you have been taught, abounding therein with thanksgiving.

COLOSSIANS 2:6–7

But without faith it is impossible to please Him: for he that comes to God must believe that He is, and that He is a rewarder of them that diligently seek Him.   HEBREWS 11:6

But if any provide not for his own, and specially for those of his own house, he has denied the faith, and is worse than an infidel.   1 TIMOTHY 5:8

Fight the good fight of faith, lay hold on eternal life, whereto you are also called, and have professed a good profession before many witnesses.   1 TIMOTHY 6:12

But continue you in the things which you have learned and have been assured of, knowing of whom you have learned them; and that from a child you have known the holy scriptures, which are able to make you wise to salvation through faith which is in Christ Jesus.   2 TIMOTHY 3:14–15

I have fought a good fight, I have finished my course, I have kept the faith.   2 TIMOTHY 4:7

INSIGHTS ON FAITH FROM SMITH WIGGLESWORTH

The Word of God is true. If you will understand the truth and right, you can be always on the line of gaining strength, overcoming oppositions, living in the world but over it, making everything subject to you.

⌒

If you listen to the Word of God this morning, it shall make you strong. You will find out that whatever work you have to do will be made easier if you keep your mind stayed on the Lord. Blessed is the man that has his mind stayed upon the Lord!

⌒

Whatever things you ask when you pray, believe that you receive them, and you will have them. Desire God, and you will have desires from God. He will meet you on the line of those desires when you reach out in simple faith.

"BELIEVE THAT GOD IS GREATER THAN YOUR HEART. BELIEVE THAT GOD IS GREATER THAN YOUR THOUGHTS. BELIEVE THAT GOD IS GREATER THAN THE DEVIL. BELIEVE THAT HE WILL PRESERVE YOU. BELIEVE IN HIS ALMIGHTINESS. AND ON THE AUTHORITY OF GOD'S FAITH IN YOU, YOU WILL TRIUMPH UNTIL HE COMES."

—SMITH WIGGLESWORTH

7

MIRACLE POWER OF FAITH

BREAKTHROUGH

And he said, The Lord *is my rock, and my fortress, and my deliverer.*   2 Samuel 22:2

For You will light my candle: the Lord *my God will enlighten my darkness. For by You I have run through a troop; and by my God have I leaped over a wall.*   Psalm 18:28–29

I will bless the Lord *at all times: His praise shall continually be in my mouth. My soul shall make her boast in the* Lord*: the humble shall hear thereof, and be glad. O magnify the* Lord *with me, and let us exalt His name together. I sought the* Lord*, and He heard me, and delivered me from all my fears. They looked to Him, and were lightened: and their faces were not ashamed. This poor man cried, and the* Lord *heard him, and saved him out of all his troubles.*   Psalm 34:1–6

The LORD is merciful and gracious, slow to anger, and plenteous in mercy. PSALM 103:8

But the mercy of the LORD is from everlasting to everlasting upon them that fear Him, and His righteousness to children's children; to such as keep His covenant, and to those that remember His commandments to do them. PSALM 103:17–18

Awake, awake; put on your strength, O Zion; put on your beautiful garments, O Jerusalem, the holy city: for hereafter there shall no more come into you the uncircumcised and the unclean. Shake yourself from the dust; arise, and sit down, O Jerusalem: loose yourself from the bands of your neck, O captive daughter of Zion. ISAIAH 52:1–2

It is of the LORD's mercies that we are not consumed, because His compassions fail not. They are new every morning: great is Your faithfulness. LAMENTATIONS 3:22–23

For thus says the LORD of hosts; Yet once, it is a little while, and I will shake the heavens, and the earth, and the sea, and the dry land; and I will shake all nations, and the desire of all nations shall come: and I will fill this house with glory, says the LORD of hosts. HAGGAI 2:6–7

The Lord your God in the midst of you is mighty; He will save, He will rejoice over you with joy; He will rest in His love, He will joy over you with singing. I will gather them that are sorrowful for the solemn assembly, who are of you, to whom the reproach of it was a burden. Behold, at that time I will undo all that afflict you: and I will save her that halts, and gather her that was driven out; and I will get them praise and fame in every land where they have been put to shame. At that time will I bring you again, even in the time that I gather you: for I will make you a name and a praise among all people of the earth, when I turn back your captivity before your eyes, says the Lord. ZEPHANIAH 3:17–20

Therefore if any man be in Christ, he is a new creature: old things are passed away; behold, all things are become new.
2 CORINTHIANS 5:17

Finally, my brethren, be strong in the Lord, and in the power of His might. EPHESIANS 6:10

Who has delivered us from the power of darkness, and has translated us into the kingdom of His dear Son. COLOSSIANS 1:13

I exhort therefore, that, first of all, supplications, prayers, intercessions, and giving of thanks, be made for all men. 1 TIMOTHY 2:1

If we confess our sins, He is faithful and just to forgive us our sins, and to cleanse us from all unrighteousness. 1 JOHN 1:9

INSIGHTS ON FAITH FROM SMITH WIGGLESWORTH

The psalmist said that he had hidden God's Word in his heart so that he might not sin against Him (Ps. 119:11). You will find that the more of God's Word you hide in your heart, the easier it is to live a holy life.

⌣

It is God's thought to make us a new creation, with all the old things passed away and all things within us truly of God; to bring in a new, divine order, a perfect love and an unlimited faith. Will you have it? Redemption is free. Arise in the activity of faith, and God will heal you as you rise. Only believe, and receive in faith.

⌣

Do you realize that if you have been created anew and born again by the Word of God that there is within you the word of power and the same light and life as the Son of God Himself had?

FAITHFULNESS

And the LORD passed by before him, and proclaimed, The LORD, the LORD God, merciful and gracious, longsuffering, and abundant in goodness and truth.   EXODUS 34:6

God is not a man, that He should lie; neither the son of man, that He should repent: has He said, and shall He not do it? or has He spoken, and shall He not make it good?   NUMBERS 23:19

Know therefore that the LORD your God, He is God, the faithful God, which keeps covenant and mercy with them that love Him and keep His commandments to a thousand generations.
                                                          DEUTERONOMY 7:9

Therefore the LORD has recompensed me according to my righteousness; according to my cleanness in His eye sight. With the merciful You will show Yourself merciful, and with the upright man You will show Yourself upright.   2 SAMUEL 22:25–26

The LORD is my light and my salvation; whom shall I fear? the LORD is the strength of my life; of whom shall I be afraid? When the wicked, even my enemies and my foes, came upon me to eat up my flesh, they stumbled and fell.   PSALM 27:1–2

For You are my rock and my fortress; therefore for Your name's sake lead me, and guide me.   PSALM 31:3

Your mercy, O LORD, is in the heavens; and Your faithfulness reaches to the clouds. PSALM 36:5

He shall send from heaven, and save me from the reproach of him that would swallow me up. Selah. God shall send forth His mercy and His truth. PSALM 57:3

I will praise You, O LORD, among the people: I will sing to You among the nations. For Your mercy is great to the heavens, and Your truth to the clouds. PSALM 57:9–10

He shall cover you with His feathers, and under His wings shall you trust: His truth shall be your shield and buckler. PSALM 91:4

For the LORD is good; His mercy is everlasting; and His truth endures to all generations. PSALM 100:5

My eyes shall be upon the faithful of the land, that they may dwell with Me: he that walks in a perfect way, he shall serve Me. He that works deceit shall not dwell within My house: he that tells lies shall not tarry in My sight. PSALM 101:6–7

For ever, O LORD, Your word is settled in heaven. Your faithfulness is to all generations: You have established the earth, and it abides. PSALM 119:89–90

Your word is true from the beginning: and every one of Your righteous judgments endures for ever. PSALM 119:160

Let not mercy and truth forsake you: bind them about your neck; write them upon the table of your heart: so shall you find favor and good understanding in the sight of God and man. PROVERBS 3:3–4

A faithful man shall abound with blessings: but he that makes haste to be rich shall not be innocent. PROVERBS 28:20

O LORD, You are my God; I will exalt You, I will praise Your name; for You have done wonderful things; Your counsels of old are faithfulness and truth. ISAIAH 25:1

His lord said to him, Well done, you good and faithful servant: you have been faithful over a few things, I will make you ruler over many things: enter you into the joy of your lord. MATTHEW 25:21

INSIGHTS ON FAITH FROM SMITH WIGGLESWORTH

Oh, it was the love of God that brought Jesus, and it is this same love that helps you and me to believe. God will be your strength in every weakness. You who need His touch, remember that He loves you. If you are wretched, helpless, or sick, look to the God of all grace, whose very essence is love, who delights to give liberally all the inheritance of life and strength and power that you are in need of.

⌒

Faith is the living principle of the Word of God. If we are led by God's Spirit, we will definitely be led into the deep things of God and His truth. The revelation of Him will be so clear that we will live by His life.

⌒

Faith is active, never dormant. Faith lays hold; faith is the hand of God; faith is the power of God. Faith never fears; faith lives amid the greatest conflict; faith is always active; faith moves even things that cannot be moved.

HEALING

There shall no evil befall you, neither shall any plague come near your dwelling. PSALM 91:10

Bless the LORD, O my soul: and all that is within me, bless His holy name. Bless the LORD, O my soul, and forget not all His benefits: who forgives all your iniquities; who heals all your diseases. PSALM 103:1–3

My son, attend to my words; incline your ear to my sayings. Let them not depart from your eyes; keep them in the midst of your heart. For they are life to those that find them, and health to all their flesh. PROVERBS 4:20–22

He gives power to the faint; and to them that have no might He increases strength. Even the youths shall faint and be weary, and the young men shall utterly fall: but they that wait upon the LORD shall renew their strength; they shall mount up with wings as eagles; they shall run, and not be weary; and they shall walk, and not faint. ISAIAH 40:29–31

And Jesus went about all Galilee, teaching in their synagogues, and preaching the gospel of the kingdom, and healing all manner of sickness and all manner of disease among the people. And His fame went throughout all Syria: and they brought to Him all sick people that were taken with divers diseases and torments, and those which were possessed with devils, and those which were lunatic, and those that had the palsy; and He healed them. MATTHEW 4:23–24

And Peter answered Him and said, Lord, if it be You, bid me come to You on the water. And He said, Come. And when Peter was come down out of the ship, he walked on the water, to go to Jesus. But when he saw the wind boisterous, he was afraid; and beginning to sink, he cried, saying, Lord, save me. And immediately Jesus stretched forth His hand, and caught him, and said to him, O you of little faith, wherefore did you doubt?

MATTHEW 14:28–31

When Jesus saw him lie, and knew that he had been now a long time in that case, He says to him, Will you be made whole?

JOHN 5:6

And they were all amazed at the mighty power of God.

LUKE 9:43

And Peter said to him, Aeneas, Jesus Christ makes you whole: arise, and make your bed. And he arose immediately.

ACTS 9:34

INSIGHTS ON FAITH FROM SMITH WIGGLESWORTH

Faith is an inward operation of that divine power that dwells in the contrite heart and can lay hold of the things not seen. Faith is a divine act; faith is God in the soul.

It is as we feed on the Word and meditate on the message it contains that the Spirit of God can vitalize what we have received and bring forth through us the word of knowledge. This word will be as full of power and life as when He, the Spirit of God, moved upon holy men in ancient times and gave them the inspired Scriptures.

Only believe, only believe, all things are possible, only believe. Only believe, only believe, all things are possible, only believe.

FAITH FOR MIRACLES

And Aaron spoke all the words which the LORD *had spoken to Moses, and did the signs in the sight of the people.* EXODUS 4:30

I would seek to God, and to God would I commit my cause: which does great things and unsearchable; marvelous things without number. JOB 5:8–9

You are the God that does wonders: You have declared Your strength among the people. PSALM 77:14

And, behold, a woman, which was diseased with an issue of blood twelve years, came behind Him, and touched the hem of His garment: for she said within herself, If I may but touch His garment, I shall be whole. But Jesus turned Him about, and when He saw her, He said, Daughter, be of good comfort; your faith has made you whole. And the woman was made whole from that hour. MATTHEW 9:20–22

And when He was come into the house, the blind men came to Him: and Jesus says to them, Believe you that I am able to do this? They said to Him, Yea, Lord. MATTHEW 9:28

And Jesus said to them, Because of your unbelief: for verily I say to you, If you have faith as a grain of mustard seed, you shall say to this mountain, Remove here to yonder place; and it shall remove; and nothing shall be impossible to you. MATTHEW 17:20

Jesus answered and said to them, Verily I say unto you, If you have faith, and doubt not, you shall not only do this which is done to the fig tree, but also if you shall say to this mountain, Be you removed, and be you cast into the sea; it shall be done. And all things, whatsoever you shall ask in prayer, believing, you shall receive. MATTHEW 21:21–22

Jesus said to him, If you can believe, all things are possible to him that believes. MARK 9:23

And these signs shall follow them that believe; in My name shall they cast out devils; they shall speak with new tongues. MARK 16:17

And they went forth, and preached every where, the Lord working with them, and confirming the word with signs following. Amen. MARK 16:20

For with God nothing shall be impossible. LUKE 1:37

Then said Jesus to him, Except you see signs and wonders, you will not believe. JOHN 4:48

Jesus answered them, I told you, and you believed not: the works that I do in My Father's name, they bear witness of Me. JOHN 10:25

INSIGHTS ON FAITH FROM SMITH WIGGLESWORTH

We are saved, called with a holy calling—called to be saints, holy, pure, Godlike, sons with power. It has been a long time now since the debt of sin was settled, our redemption was secured, and death was abolished. Mortality is a hindrance, but death no longer has power. Sin no longer has dominion. You reign in Christ; you appropriate His finished work. Don't groan and travail for a week if you are in need; *"only believe"* (Mark 5:36). Don't fight to get some special thing; *"only believe."* It is according to your faith that you will receive. God blesses you with faith. *"Have faith in God"* (Mark 11:22). If you are free in God, believe, and it will come to pass.

To believe is to have the knowledge of Him in whom you believe. It is not to believe in the word Jesus, but to believe in the nature of Christ, to believe in the vision of Christ, for all power has been given unto Him, and greater is He who is within you in the revelation of faith than he who is in the world.

God wants you to have a pure, active faith so that all the time, you will be living in an advanced place of believing God, and you will be on the mountaintop and singing when other people are crying.

FAITH FOR MIRACLES

Jesus says to her, Said I not to you, that, if you would believe, you should see the glory of God? Then they took away the stone from the place where the dead was laid. And Jesus lifted up His eyes, and said, Father, I thank You that You have heard Me. And I knew that You hear me always: but because of the people which stand by I said it, that they may believe that You have sent Me.

JOHN 11:40–42

Then Peter said, Silver and gold have I none; but such as I have give I you: in the name of Jesus Christ of Nazareth rise up and walk.

ACTS 3:6

By stretching forth Your hand to heal; and that signs and wonders may be done by the name of Your holy child Jesus.

ACTS 4:30

Long time therefore abode they speaking boldly in the Lord, which gave testimony to the word of His grace, and granted signs and wonders to be done by their hands.

ACTS 14:3

And this did she many days. But Paul, being grieved, turned and said to the spirit, I command you in the name of Jesus Christ to come out of her. And he came out the same hour.

ACTS 16:18

Moreover it is required in stewards, that a man be found faithful.

1 CORINTHIANS 4:2

Now there are diversities of gifts, but the same Spirit. And there are differences of administrations, but the same Lord. And there are diversities of operations, but it is the same God which works all in all.   1 CORINTHIANS 12:4–6

And God has set some in the church, first apostles, secondarily prophets, thirdly teachers, after that miracles, then gifts of healings, helps, governments, diversities of tongues.
                    1 CORINTHIANS 12:28

For all the promises of God in Him are yea, and in Him Amen, to the glory of God by us.   2 CORINTHIANS 1:20

Neglect not the gift that is in you, which was given you by prophecy, with the laying on of the hands of the presbytery.
                    1 TIMOTHY 4:14

Wherefore I put you in remembrance that you stir up the gift of God, which is in you by the putting on of my hands.
                    2 TIMOTHY 1:6

If we believe not, yet He abides faithful: He cannot deny Himself.   2 TIMOTHY 2:13

Behold, we count them happy which endure. You have heard of the patience of Job, and have seen the end of the Lord; that the Lord is very pitiful, and of tender mercy.   JAMES 5:11

INSIGHTS ON FAITH FROM SMITH WIGGLESWORTH

I maintain that, by the grace of God, we are so rich, we are so abounding, we have such a treasure-house, we have such a storehouse of God, we have such an unlimited faith to share in all that God has, for it is ours. We are the cream of the earth; we are the precious fruit of the earth.

Faith is the victory. Faith is the operation in your heart. Faith is the stimulation of the life of the Master. Faith is the position where God takes you to the place where you are over all by the power of God.

Some are anxious because, when they are prayed for, the thing that they are expecting does not happen that same night. They say they believe, but you can see that they are really in turmoil from their unbelief. Abraham believed God. You can hear him saying to Sarah, "Sarah, there is no life in you, and there is nothing in me; but God has promised us a son, and I believe God." That kind of faith is a joy to our Father in heaven.

POWER FOR MIRACLES

And He humbled you, and allowed you to hunger, and fed you with manna, which you knew not, neither did your fathers know; that He might make you know that man does not live by bread only, but by every word that proceeds out of the mouth of the LORD does man live.   DEUTERONOMY 8:3

Verily, verily, I say to you, He that believes on Me, the works that I do shall he do also; and greater works than these shall he do; because I go to My Father.   JOHN 14:12

However when He, the Spirit of truth, is come, He will guide you into all truth: for He shall not speak of Himself; but whatsoever He shall hear, that shall He speak: and He will show you things to come.   JOHN 16:13

You men of Israel, hear these words; Jesus of Nazareth, a man approved of God among you by miracles and wonders and signs, which God did by Him in the midst of you, as you yourselves also know.   ACTS 2:22

And His name through faith in His name has made this man strong, whom you see and know: yea, the faith which is by Him has given him this perfect soundness in the presence of you all.   ACTS 3:16

Then Philip went down to the city of Samaria, and preached Christ to them. And the people with one accord gave heed to those things which Philip spoke, hearing and seeing the miracles which he did.   ACTS 8:5–6

And God wrought special miracles by the hands of Paul: so that from his body were brought to the sick handkerchiefs or aprons, and the diseases departed from them, and the evil spirits went out of them.   ACTS 19:11–12

And God has both raised up the LORD, and will also raise up us by His own power.   1 CORINTHIANS 6:14

But covet earnestly the best gifts: and yet show I to you a more excellent way.   1 CORINTHIANS 12:31

For we walk by faith, not by sight.   2 CORINTHIANS 5:7

Truly the signs of an apostle were wrought among you in all patience, in signs, and wonders, and mighty deeds.   2 CORINTHIANS 12:12

He therefore that ministers to you the Spirit, and works miracles among you, does He it by the works of the law, or by the hearing of faith?   GALATIANS 3:5

Therefore we ought to give the more earnest heed to the things which we have heard, lest at any time we should let them slip.

HEBREWS 2:1

Submit yourselves therefore to God. Resist the devil, and he will flee from you. Draw near to God, and He will draw near to you. Cleanse your hands, you sinners; and purify your hearts, you double minded.

JAMES 4:7–8

Is any sick among you? let him call for the elders of the church; and let them pray over him, anointing him with oil in the name of the Lord: and the prayer of faith shall save the sick, and the Lord shall raise him up; and if he have committed sins, they shall be forgiven him. Confess your faults one to another, and pray one for another, that you may be healed. The effectual fervent prayer of a righteous man avails much.

JAMES 5:14–16

And whatsoever we ask, we receive of Him, because we keep His commandments, and do those things that are pleasing in His sight.

1 JOHN 3:22

INSIGHTS ON FAITH FROM SMITH WIGGLESWORTH

Dare to believe God; He will not fail. Faith is the greatest subject; in it is power to lay hold of the Word of God. It is God who brings us into victory through the blood of the slain Lamb. Faith quickens us into a divine order, a living new source, a holy nature, having divine rights through Jesus.

⌒

Faith always brings a fact, and a fact brings joy. Faith! Faith! Making us know that God exists, *"and that He is a rewarder of those who diligently seek Him"* (Heb. 11:6). *"God, who gives life to the dead and calls those things which do not exist as though they did"* (Rom. 4:17). Those who trust God lack nothing. He gives life to the dead.

⌒

My faith pure, my joy sure.

RECEIVING A MIRACLE

And said, If you will diligently hearken to the voice of the Lord *your God, and will do that which is right in His sight, and will give ear to His commandments, and keep all His statutes, I will put none of these diseases upon you, which I have brought upon the Egyptians: for I am the* Lord *that heals you.*

Exodus 15:26

Commit your way to the Lord*; trust also in Him; and He shall bring it to pass.*

Psalm 37:5

Surely He has borne our griefs, and carried our sorrows: yet we did esteem Him stricken, smitten of God, and afflicted. But He was wounded for our transgressions, He was bruised for our iniquities: the chastisement of our peace was upon Him; and with His stripes we are healed.

Isaiah 53:4–5

The Lord *is good to them that wait for Him, to the soul that seeks Him.*

Lamentations 3:25

How precious also are Your thoughts to me, O God! how great is the sum of them! If I should count them, they are more in number than the sand: when I awake, I am still with You.

Psalm 139:17–18

And when Jesus came into the ruler's house, and saw the minstrels and the people making a noise, He said to them, Give place: for the maid is not dead, but sleeps. And they laughed Him to scorn. But when the people were put forth, He went in, and took her by the hand, and the maid arose. And the fame hereof went abroad into all that land.   MATTHEW 9:23–26

As soon as Jesus heard the word that was spoken, He said to the ruler of the synagogue, Be not afraid, only believe.   MARK 5:36

For verily I say to you, that whosoever shall say to this mountain, Be you removed, and be you cast into the sea; and shall not doubt in his heart, but shall believe that those things which he says shall come to pass; he shall have whatsoever he says.   MARK 11:23

For therein is the righteousness of God revealed from faith to faith: as it is written, The just shall live by faith.   ROMANS 1:17

And hope makes not ashamed; because the love of God is shed abroad in our hearts by the Holy Ghost which is given to us.
ROMANS 5:5

For we are saved by hope: but hope that is seen is not hope: for what a man sees, why does he yet hope for? But if we hope for that we see not, then do we with patience wait for it.
ROMANS 8:24–25

Jesus Christ the same yesterday, and to day, and for ever.

HEBREWS 13:8

If any of you lack wisdom, let him ask of God, that gives to all men liberally, and upbraids not; and it shall be given him. But let him ask in faith, nothing wavering. For he that wavers is like a wave of the sea driven with the wind and tossed. For let not that man think that he shall receive any thing of the Lord.   JAMES 1:5–7

For as the body without the spirit is dead, so faith without works is dead also.   JAMES 2:26

Submit yourselves therefore to God. Resist the devil, and he will flee from you.   JAMES 4:7

Who His own self bare our sins in His own body on the tree, that we, being dead to sins, should live to righteousness: by whose stripes you were healed.   1 PETER 2:24

For whatsoever is born of God overcomes the world: and this is the victory that overcomes the world, even our faith.

1 JOHN 5:4

"GOD HAS A PERFECT WORK FOR US, A HEARING OF FAITH. WHEN WE HAVE THE HEARING OF FAITH, WE ARE WITHIN THE SOUND OF HIS VOICE, AND WHEN WE HEAR HIM SPEAK, WE FIND THAT OUR OWN SPEECH BETRAYS US. WITH THIS HEARING OF FAITH, WE ARE EPISTLES OF THE DIVINE CHARACTER, HAVING HIS LIFE, PASSION, AND COMPASSION. BELOVED, THERE MUST BE THIS DIVINE FELLOWSHIP BETWEEN US AND GOD."

—SMITH WIGGLESWORTH

MY FAVORITE BIBLE PROMISES

The Greatest Bible Promises for Healing and Comfort

There is comfort in knowing that the hardest things are just lifting places into the grace of God. He is our Deliverer. This collection of Scripture promises helps the reader understand that, in these times, God wants to bring us through our needs and into the victory He has for us. Wigglesworth's wisdom helps us learn to let go of our challenges and see God take hold and hold us up.

The Greatest Bible Promises for the Anointing and Power of the Holy Spirit

God never made mankind to be a failure. He wants us to know the truth in such a way that we have a clear understanding of what it means to receive the power of the Holy Spirit. This compilation of Bible promises combined with the wisdom of Wigglesworth will help readers realize that the anointing of the Holy Spirit brings God's best for their lives.

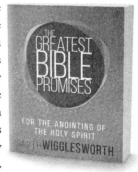

The Smith Wigglesworth quotes throughout this book were taken from the following Whitaker House published titles...

Smith Wigglesworth on Faith
978-0-88368-531-0

> Faith is a gift of God that is available to all who will receive it.

Smith Wigglesworth: The Power of Faith
978-0-88368-608-9

> The sustaining effect of the smallest drop of faith will create continual ripples of power.

Smith Wigglesworth on Ever Increasing Faith
978-0-88368-633-1

> Join the evangelist in the great adventure called "faith."

Smith Wigglesworth on the Power of Scripture
978-1-60374-094-4

> You will cherish this glimpse into the heart and mind of one of God's most gifted servants.

Smith Wigglesworth on the Anointing
978-0-88368-530-3

> As you live in His anointing, your spiritual life will become more fruitful.

Smith Wigglesworth on the Holy Spirit
978-0-88368-544-0

> Learn how the fullness of the Holy Spirit can be yours.

Smith Wigglesworth on Healing
978-0-88368-426-9

> Not only can you be healed of your sicknesses, but God can use you to bring healing to others.

Smith Wigglesworth on Spiritual Gifts
978-0-88368-533-4

> You can be the instrument God uses to transmit His love and miracles to others.

Smith Wigglesworth on Heaven
978-0-88368-954-7

> Discover God's plans for you in this life and what He has in store for you in the heaven.

The beloved, classic KJV text with its language updated to modern equivalents without any doctrinal changes.

In this translation, the trusted KJV text remains doctrinally intact, but its archaic language and difficult words have been replaced for clarity with their modern equivalents.

This Bible is also a complete red letter edition, meaning that the direct words of God are indicated in red in both the Old and New Testaments–currently the only Bible with this feature.

If you want to pass along the KJV that you know and love to the next generation of believers without compromising the translation that you trust, the KJVER is the Bible for you.

The Trusted King James in an Easy Read Format ™

whitakerhouse.com/kjver